HE REVIV WITH APRICOTS

*Excerpts from each Psalm
for Meditation and Healing*

BOOK ONE   Psalms 1-51

John York Moore

1

SONG OF SONGS 2.5

'He refreshed me with raisins: he revived me with apricots.' (NEB)

For Emily and in memory of Helen who 'etched happy memories on many hearts'.

First published 2013 by John York Moore, 9 Larrigan Crescent, Penzance. TR18 9NH

2nd impression

Distributed by St Mary's Church, Penzance. TR18 4AQ

ISBN 978-0-9930018-0-2

Artwork by Stella Maris, www.stellamarisartist.com

Printed by Headland Printers Ltd., Penzance.

INDEX

FOREWORD

Dr. John York Moore has given his readers a very great gift. His translation of the Psalms into the Haiku format reasserts their beauty and poetic verbal power.

His words are simple, direct and comforting and bring a fresh relevance and devotional potency to this ancient vehicle of praise and worship. Across three millennia these verses have been cried afresh, in joy, in hope, in fear and in pain. Today, our voices join in that communion as we seek the Lord in the fast-flowing waters of life.

With his personal background and experience as a GP and as an Anglican Franciscan Tertiary, Dr York Moore brings to his work the insight and empathy of the healer and the devotional commitment and discipline of the monastic Divine Office (the eight hours of each day and night at which prayer is offered up). He also shares his tremendous kindness and generosity of spirit, combined with a care and tolerance that pervades the pages of his commentary.

Along the journey, signposts are placed to help the reader, indicating words of Scripture or other helpful texts to be read, music to be experienced and practical exercises to assist contemplative prayer. John, we your readers thank you.

Michelle P. Brown
Professor Emerita of Medieval Manuscript Studies
School of Advanced Study
University of London.
Former Lay Canon of St. Paul's Cathedral, London

The Purpose of this Book

'Happy is he who has found Wisdom, she is a staff of Life to all who grasp her, and those who hold her fast are safe.' Proverbs 3.13 & 18.

When medieval Jews made their wills, there were two parts. The first part dealt with possessions, the second contained words of wisdom for their offspring. The Psalms are an ancient source of wisdom – addressing universal human issues. They may seem an unlikely source of help in the twenty-first century but human nature, and God's love for humanity, remain unchanged. I believe the Psalms have words of wisdom for everyone, whatever they believe.

Some years ago my wife, Helen, who has since died, looked for a book about the Psalms to give to our grand-daughter Emily. Emily was about to be confirmed in her Christian faith and Helen could not find the right book. I offered to write one and the seed for this publication was sown. I hope to bring out the wisdom of the Psalms in a new way. To achieve this I have amended the old texts to make them accessible for our time. I have replaced negative ideas with upbeat ones and tempered hostile themes without losing their meaning and significance.

Some of my ideas you may think wrong. If so, ask God to show you what plans He has for you. His Divine Love will show you where to go. *'Do not think we are dictating the terms of your faith; your hold on the faith is secure enough.'* These words come from 2 Corinthians 1.24.

Most of us crave meaning in Life. Saint Augustine said *'You made us for yourself O Lord, and our hearts are restless till they rest in You'.* There are many religions in the world. In this country we find a widespread dissatisfaction with the way Christianity is presented. At the same time there is a longing for some form of spirituality. I believe God has a unique purpose for each person, whether Christian or not.

Contemplative Prayer has been my life-line since 1938. I know that meditation can help everyone. I have suggested suitable exercises in the Appendices 2 and 3. Those with 'alternative' beliefs will have to find another word for God. Just as the body and mind need feeding, so our spirits need regular food. The Book of Psalms is one way God provides this.

With God as our shepherd we lack nothing; our devotional larder overflows. The text of the Psalms can be transformed into a life-giving spring of healing and joy. When its loving ideas are combined with the message of the New Testament, they comfort you and 'give you strength' - the original meaning of comfort. They will nourish you from dawn to dusk and during the night.

Looking back on my own life, I now see that God started to nourish me at a very tender age. The first service that I recall going to was at Easter when about five. I remember how much I was thrilled by hearing 'Alleluia'. I drew in my breath, making a loud hissing noise of approval, every time it was sung. I did not then know it meant *'Praise the Lord'.*

The process of reading and absorbing all this spiritual material can be compared with eating dried apricots. Proper cooking makes them taste better - but it takes time.

INTRODUCTION

'The best way to defend the faith is to show how old truths can be translated into modern language.' Bede Griffiths[1]

Background

The Psalms are a set of poems. They record the legends and history of the Hebrew People from 1800 BC to 520 BC. During this time the Hebrew people lived on the coast-line of the Eastern Mediterranean. They spread to Egypt and Babylon where they were enslaved.

Most of the Psalms were written between 1000 BC and 500 BC. Parts of Psalm 105 are close to the *Hymn to the Sun* of the Pharaoh Akhnaten. At this time the concept of one God developed. Other Psalms update the beliefs of those who followed Ba'al. The number and order of the Psalms were decided about 200 BC and they tell of growth in the Knowledge of God. Meanwhile Hinduism had become more refined and other beliefs such as Taoism and Buddhism had appeared. By the time Jesus was born these other religions had reached the region. One of Jesus' prayer patterns was to repeat simple words many times. Buddhist practice also uses repetition in the form of mantras.

Using This Version of the Psalms

1. The excerpts from The Psalms are concentrated. They should be consumed sparingly or you might get Spiritual Indigestion and give up. Look at difficult passages later.
2. The refrain and first paragraph of text give the core

meaning of the psalm.

3. You may find it helps to read the psalm that you intend to study in another version first.

4. The psalm numbers correspond with those in the Book of Common Prayer.

The Style of the Psalms in this Book

I present the Psalms in an epic Japanese poetic style known as *renga*. This alternates between stanzas of three and two lines.

The first stanza uses five syllables in the first and last lines and seven syllables in the middle. This is a Haiku. Originally these poems were about the seasons. The second stanza has two lines of seven syllables. In the Haiku tradition the two parts are related, as are the verses of the Psalms with two contrasting sections. Eastern and Western traditions are thus closely linked.

In religious houses, when a psalm is said there is a pause in the middle of each stanza (marked with a colon) for about two seconds. This is the time to take a breath. I was once advised that the pause should last long enough to say *'Jesus'*. If even more time is allowed, and the words are said very slowly indeed, as in private prayer, they sink into the Ground of our Being.

UPPER CASE LETTERS are used when Jehovah is addressed in the original Hebrew as FATHER or GOD and to denote the twelve GRACES (see pages 15-17).

Comments

Opposite each psalm there are comments including references to other psalms and other parts of both Testaments. I offer my own interpretations of the material as well as quotations from a wide range of people. As a retired GP, many of my own connections inevitably relate to health and well-being.

A Description of God

Adjectives are used to describe the nature of things or people. For those who believe there is a God, His essence is that He cannot be limited by language. He is ineffable – He cannot be understood. Even the word 'He' is limiting; it ascribes gender. For convenience I shall continue to use it rather than S/He. However, in some psalms, which I shall indicate, the feminine element is more important.

He is Infinite.

He is all powerful – Omnipotent. As will be seen, we are given Power; there is good reason. When we use this as He has planned for us, we become His children.

He knows everything – He is Omniscient.

He is everywhere – He is Omnipresent.

He has existed before time began, and will survive beyond the end of time – He is Eternal.

These are difficult words for modern usage. When, and if, you meditate with these excerpts from the Psalms, you may prefer to use other words.

God's Graces - the Building Blocks of Heaven

The word 'Psalms' means 'Songs of Praise'. They 'Give Thanks to God' for the Graces that are passed on to human-beings at conception. Then they act as the invisible effect of the Divine upon each of us. The Graces describe what God is like in an active, dynamic, sense, but never completely. They draw us into a perfect relationship with the Trinity. A similar type of belief is found in Judaism, Islam, and in some Eastern religions.[2] St. Paul compares these Graces to clothes that we should put on.[3]

The Graces vary with different translations and they abound in the Psalms. I refer to twelve : LIFE, LOVE, WISDOM, RIGHTEOUSNESS, KNOWLEDGE, GOODNESS, TRUTH, POWER, GLORY, HOLINESS, JOY, PEACE.

LIFE The Holy Spirit breathes Life into souls at conception.[4] Breathing does not start until after birth.

LOVE In Greek there are four words for Love. 'Agape' means Divine Love, the kind of love that overcomes evil. However, this type of love can involve suffering - The Virgin Mary[5] and Christ both suffered. So did Aslan in Narnia, and Harry Potter's mother.[6] Jesus says *'I give you a new commandment, that you love one another. Just as I have loved you, you also should love one another. By this everyone will know that you are my disciples, if you have love for one*

15

another.' (John13.34-35)

WISDOM was created first of all. In Psalm 14 God searches the world for those wise enough to accept Him.

RIGHTEOUSNESS is a difficult word, often misunderstood. One commentary for Psalm 85, The Gelineau *Singing Version of the Psalms,* suggests it is *'the loving purpose of God for all human-kind'.* Jesus is the embodiment of this purpose.

KNOWLEDGE accompanies Wisdom and Respect for the Lord; fools scorn Wisdom – Psalm 14.

GOODNESS is the way we reveal God's Love towards other people. Roald Dahl says in *The Twits, 'A person who has good thoughts can never be ugly. ... good thoughts will shine out of your face like sunbeams.'*

TRUTH Sincerity and integrity are the hall-marks of good behaviour. One must sometimes be careful when telling the Truth. Love must take priority so that people do not feel guilt or other hurt. Divine love is alert and avoids harm.

POWER or strength is the Grace that God has given to human-kind that allows us free-will. We are not robots. By giving us the power of choice He is no longer Omnipotent. He has surrendered some of His Power to us. We have the ability to do things that are evil. Evil is not of His making, it is ours. When we surrender our free-will back to Him His Omnipotence is restored and we have the Power to become Sons of God.

God's GLORY is seen in the sky every day and night. The

radiant splendour of the Birth and Transfiguration of Christ caused awe in those who were witnesses.

HOLINESS is a word with two meanings - being 'set apart' and 'without blemish.' Healing and wholeness are closely related.

JOY[7] is a by-product of the Graces. To attain one's Heart's Desire and Forgiveness – given or received – brings Joy.

PEACE is the calm that follows disorder.

All of the Graces are God's gift to us; our Heart's Desire is our proper response to these gifts. When these two combine, His Light shines upon the world.

The Psalms and Prayer

The Psalms are a profound source of Knowledge. They are presented in a way that is simple but strong. When the sweet aroma of the creative ones is distilled, the harshness of the bitter ones is laid bare. Rather than reject these I have transformed them into something meaningful and good.[8]

The Psalms teach us how to pray throughout Life, even when we are dying. Jesus used Psalm 22 on the Cross, twice.

Different Types of Prayer

Saint Francis de Sales used a floral metaphor for meditation. In *Introduction to the Devout Life* he compares it to walking through a lovely garden where one is allowed to pick the flowers. He wrote *'no one would want to leave without taking a bunch of blooms to remind themselves of it later in the* day'. Gardens always need attention. Prayer needs to be continuous to be fully effective.

For <u>Saint Teresa of Avila</u> there are four types of prayer. She relates different types to methods of watering a garden.

1. The hardest type is like going down into a water-source with a bucket. You carry it and take it to the plants
   - this is work - you make up prayers as you go.

2. A windlass using an animal which does the work
   - using prayers composed by someone else.

3. A stream can be diverted; the Lord supplies the water. Your existing thoughts are nourished by His input
   - the type of prayer suggested here as meditation.

4. Rain comes down from heaven. You do nothing (except murmur a little word such as GOD or LOVE)[9] God takes charge.
   - this is Contemplation.

An Example of How to Meditate and Contemplate

<u>Posture</u> Sit comfortably and upright, otherwise you may go to sleep. You may find a prayer stool, multiple cushions, or even the 'lotus position' suits you. If not, a chair with a straight back is fine. Hands resting on your lap, lightly cupped with the fingers of one hand supporting the other and thumbs touching. Have both feet on the floor and take your shoes off.

Breathing Take gentle movements when breathing in and out. Abdominal movements allow the lower parts of your lungs to be expanded. Practice breathing in for a slow count of five, breathing out slowly until nine is reached, and pausing at ten, before starting again. Breathing then corresponds to one's natural rhythm. As described it is not a religious exercise, though I believe God through His Love will give help to those who choose to meditate in this way. See page 138.

Be aware that God is in this place, waiting for you with Love. Spend time with this thought and with each member of the Trinity. Then think of Him as Father, Son, and Her[10] as Holy Spirit. Spend time with each member of the Trinity. Make the Sign of the Cross physically or mentally. Use generous movements - the Trinity is generous to you. Ask the Spirit to guide you. She works entirely in your favour. An extended version of this is to be found on page 139.

Before I begin contemplation I set a kitchen timer to ring at the end of the allotted time.[11]

Jesus used two sorts of prayer. Firstly, when immediate action was called for, such as feeding five thousand. Secondly, meditating by repeating a simple phrase - a mantra - for several hours when strength was needed. For this He would go away to a lonely place, as in Mark 6.46, sometimes spending all night there (Luke 6.12) likewise when surrender to His Father's Will was the purpose, as in Gethsemane. Congregational prayer is the first type. Private prayer, meditation and contemplation correspond with the second. Having used Contemplative Exercises for so long, I delight in this form of prayer. We can use it to promote the way God's Graces grow in us. Then we shall become the person He created us to be.

Few teachers of prayer understand how human nervous and immune systems operate; this knowledge would help them greatly. Adrenalin and Cortisone are secreted by the Adrenal Glands. The Conscious and Sympathetic Systems use Adrenalin; the hormone causes wear and tear. Large amounts stimulate the body in an emergency. The Sub-conscious, Parasympathetic System, which works best when we rest sleep or pray, repairs the damage. This hormone is Cortisone. Twenty minutes elapse before healing dis-ease is under way. Our bodies can be damaged by some emotions - guilt, resentment and anger all interfere with our immune responses and impair health. Psalm 6 elaborates on this theme.

Regular slow breaths and the use of a mantra will assist meditation. I like to relate breathing with God's Graces. On breathing in, a Grace is drawn into my being; exhaling gives it to the world. I aim to develop calmness and smile at life's problems.[12] A positive approach adds years to one's life.

Lectio Divina - Divine Reading

'Seek in reading, find in meditation, knock in prayer, enter through contemplation.' Guigo the Carthusian.[13]

The Collect for the Last Sunday after Trinity in the Church of England Lectionary advises us 'to read, mark, learn, and inwardly digest' biblical readings. Thus there are four stages.

Lectio Divina has four stages. Matthew 7.7-8 is similar.

For me, before I start any form of biblical reading or prayer, at any time of day or night, I pause awhile. I spend about two minutes doing nothing except becoming aware that I am in the presence of God. He is waiting for me, and welcomes me with Love. I need to 'be still and know' God the Father is here, God the Son is here, and so is God the Holy Spirit. Then :

1. We read [*seek*] the words.

2. We meditate on a theme - we mark [*find*] them.

3. We pray [*knock*] to God about them, and in the process learn his desire for us.

4. We inwardly digest them [they *enter* us]. Our bodies, mind and Spirit are warmed as we dwell *within* God - Contemplation. We discover that God needs us as much as we need Him - Song of Songs 7.10 '*I am my Beloved's and His desire is for me.*' We are filled with Joy and transformed by the Holy Spirit.

5. We return to our work and may make a resolution.

To fit prayer into a busy routine requires skill. There may be enough time to do only one step in any one day. Once this becomes a habit, life's problems can be handed over to God when we feel lost.

The Psalms and Healing

God loves us very, very, very, very much. He wants us to talk to him, and ask his advice. For me, because I was a General Practitioner, He is the perfect healer. I think of sin as a cancer, and God is the most skilful surgeon I can imagine. He will transform a human-being with mortal sins into a healthy person. He will do it in a way that causes least distress even if the cause was one's own fault. He will show Understanding and Love[14] and we shall be whole. Dis-ease will have gone. His Love never fails us, even though we fail Him.

When praying for healing of ourselves or others we must ask God the Father to operate in the way He sees best. Then our prayers accord with His will. The Collect for the Tenth Sunday after Trinity reminds us that our petition will be granted.

The Psalms and Sleep

Sleep is the natural way our bodies and our minds repair daily wear and tear. The repair process starts after about twenty minutes rest, even if not actually asleep. Restlessness and anxiety interfere with its action.

Three points deserve attention specially when prayer is being used to encourage sleep.

1. One may notice sudden unintentional breaths being taken. This is a precursor to sleep when the breathing centre of the brain takes command of respiration.

2. One may be woken up by a sudden, violent twitch, specially early in the night. This also does not matter. This time it means one has gone to sleep. There is no need for panic, just

be glad, *'Be still and know'* sleep is not far away.

3. Very occasionally, mostly in the morning hours, there is a lovely warm feeling spreading all over one's body. This is a cause for joy. Again, sleep is not far away.

The Psalms and God's Purpose for Us

In Psalm 8 three questions are raised about God and mankind.

1. *'Why do we exist?'* - God made us. We each have a part in His Divine Plan for the universe as if we are in the Garden of Eden. The seeds of His Graces are sown in each human being at conception and grow according to our abilities and desires as in the parable of the sheep and goats. If our Heart's Desire is for their maximum yield, we will ask the Head Gardener, God, for help. He becomes our guide and teacher, walks with us through His garden and blesses us so that we become a blessing to the world. Prayer will help us to discover the nature of that blessing.

The psalm tells us that God has given us power (dominion over) the creatures He has made. The power to do evil is ours. He remains Omniscient, Omnipresent, Infinite and Eternal. By returning our power to God we share in His Omnipotence as co-creators in the world, and can work miracles on His behalf. The Graces grow in us and become part of our Nature. We will solve our problems by showing Divine Love and Wisdom in our actions. *'Then we shall not hurt or destroy in all God's Holy mountain and the land shall be filled with knowledge of the Lord as the waters cover the sea'* (Isaiah 11.9).

2. *'How do we relate to God?'* In different ways, but we all need Him. 2 Peter 1.4 tells us that God wants us to share His Divine nature and to Love others as we Love ourselves. When we respect ourselves we learn to respect others. Contemplative Prayer will show us the best way to demonstrate that Love.

3. *'How do we know when we are doing the right thing with our free-will?'* It is all to do with our 'Heart's Desire'. God allows us to do whatever we ask - 2 Corinthians 1.19. To ensure that other people benefit from our actions and do His Will requires that we act with Love - Divine Love. (In *All Hallows' Eve,* a poignant story about the struggle between Good and Evil, Charles Williams brings out this point.) It is our personal responsibility to surrender our bodies, minds and spirits to Him through prayer and in our lives. Evil is not of His making, it is ours. He will help us to eliminate it, but not necessarily in the way we would choose.

The Jesus Prayer

The version I use most is :
Lord Jesus Christ have mercy on me.[15]
I breathe in while saying *'Lord Jesus Christ have'*, breathe out with *'mercy on me'*, and rest. (See Appendix 2. Coping with Modern Life 2)

Other versions are:
Lord Jesus Christ, Son of God:
have mercy on me, a sinner.[16]
and
Lord Jesus Christ, the Son of God:
Have mercy on me, pardon my misdeeds.

In Greek, the Prayer has twenty-four syllables. A version with the same number of syllables is in the comments for Psalm 30. All can be used as a mantra - said repeatedly. The process is assisted by using a knotted prayer cord.[17] This has one hundred knots with a marker every twenty-five. For practical purposes use 'worry beads'. They often have a circle of twenty-five and are convenient for ordinary use.

The Jesus Prayer can be used as a formal prayer, when walking or when awake at night.

The Prayer has precursors in the Psalms: 6.4, 25.10, 30.1-3, 41.4, 51.1. The first and fourth are very elegant. The last, in the original Hebrew, is maternal towards human-kind but there are hints of this side of God's nature in other Psalms e.g. 40.13, 51.1.

We can see ourselves in God's eyes as the field that contained buried treasure (Matthew 13.44) or in my metaphor as the most choice apricot on the tree.

Learning from Other Faiths

To grow spiritually will involve changing our nature and being ready to expand our ideas, and, as Turkish novelist Elif Shafak has said, to learn from people who are different from ourselves.[18] Elif is a Sufi Moslem; she is dedicated to Mysticism. Christians have much that they can learn from her novels and from Islamic principles. Its members pray five times a day, they fast severely during Ramadan and they go on

Pilgrimage to Mecca at least once in their lifetime. The Mihrab, a niche in a mosque which points to Mecca, is sometimes dedicated to the Virgin Mary. The Hagia Sophia in Istanbul, now a museum, is a good example.

Allah has ninety-nine Beautiful Names; many reflect the Graces used in this book.

The Society of Saint Francis, an Anglican Community, believes strongly that the integrity of belief in those of different faiths should be left intact. Franciscans observe this aim.[19] Their Rule of Life was written at Poona in an Ashram - a Hindu religious community - in about 1922. Its members were English Christians; their adaptation to the Indian way of life included dress. The community still exists. It offers accommodation for Hindu, Muslim, and Christian students.

Bede Griffiths, a Jesuit, lived at a Hindu Ashram only a few miles away, as a man of prayer (Sannyasi). He had been there nearly forty years when he died in 1993.

Thomas Merton (1915-1968) a Catholic Trappist, studied Buddhism. He wrote *'The Eastern religions have the advantage of disposing man more naturally for contemplation'.*[20] T.N. Hanh, a Buddhist, seeks to strengthen, not change, Christian belief.

Meister Eckhart (1260-1328) a German theologian and mystic, is widely admired. Protestants and Catholics, Buddhists and Hindus, believers and unbelievers, as well as the psychologist C. G. Jung, all respond to him.[21]

In considering the value of other faiths we must of course remember that the Psalms are Jewish in origin.

Anglicans can find a great deal about Christian belief from Roman Catholic literature without having to agree with all Catholic doctrines. We can even learn from atheists who love to tell us about our failings!

At all stages of belief it is good to know someone experienced in prayer, with whom progress can be discussed, preferably at least twice a year.

Abbreviations

- BCP   Book of Common Prayer
- JB   Jerusalem Bible
- JBR   Jerusalem Bible, The Psalms for Reading or Recitation (Darton, Longman & Todd, 1969)
- KJB   King James Bible
- NEB   New English Bible
- NRSV   New Revised Standard Version
- NTE   New Testament for Everyone (SPCK, 2011)
- PfP   Psalms for Praying
- SJ   Songs for the Journey, The Psalms in Life and Liturgy (Darton, Longman & Todd, 2002)
- Taizé   Psalms from Taizé (Mowbray, 1983)
- TP   The Psalms, Singing Version (Fontana, 1966) (Gelineau)

Psalms 1 - 51

1   **Life with (and without) God**

Refrain ℜ   *Blest is the soul whose JOY it*
                is : to walk the Way of GOD.

    Bless-ed is the soul :
    whose counsel is to walk the
    Way of God the LORD.
        Her JOY is in His Word : she
        ponders on it day and night.   ℜ

    She is like a tree
    beside a stream : and yields her
    fruit at harvest time.
        Ungodliness shall fail : and
        rogues walk Ways of RIGHTEOUSNESS. ℜ

The first two words of the first psalm - *'Blessed is'* - draw us immediately to Jesus' teaching in the Sermon on the Mount[22] where He lists the qualities of those who are *'Blessed'*.

It is good to find a reason to refer to the New Testament and to Jesus Christ so early in the Psalms. The 'Way' reminds us that Jesus referred to Himself as *'the Way'* - God's example for us.

There is then a change of gender in the psalm - from male to female. The word for Spirit/Soul is female in Hebrew, in Greek (psyche) and in Latin (anima).

The second half of the psalm refers to the fate of the *'ungodly'*. We all fail to live up to God's standards. Peter failed Jesus at His Passion when he denied Him.[23] After the Resurrection, by the lakeside, Peter's threefold denial was forgiven.[24] His penance was a threefold affirmation of friendship for Jesus. The *'way to doom'* was averted and Peter became the leader of the Church.

The word *Righteousness* can feel onerous but when it is interpreted as *'God's Loving purpose for human-kind'*[25] it falls into place.

There is great comfort in this psalm, as well as direction for us in our lives today.

2   The Father's Chosen King

Refrain ℜ   *Why scorn the LORD? : Learn WISDOM,*
          trust in Him, be filled with JOY.

Unbelievers : why
do you reject the LORD and
His anointed King?
        The LORD said : 'I enthroned Him
        on My hill of HOLINESS.   ℜ

You are now My Son :
I have begotten You, and
You shall rule the world.'
        Learn KNOWLEDGE, WISDOM, serve and
        trust the LORD : be filled with JOY.   ℜ

This psalm was used at the enthronement of a king. The royal palace was next to the Temple and the king was both ruler and God's Power on earth. In the Old Testament, 1 Samuel records how Saul was anointed king and how David was anointed by Samuel while Saul was still alive. Throughout Saul's reign David regarded Saul's life as sacred, even when his own life was in danger.

Jesus was of David's line. It was in Zion (a designation for David's City) that Jesus met death. He was the Lord's Anointed One. His temple was His body in which He was the Divine King. Pilate acted against his better will; Jesus' Divine Graces were ignored, His body flogged,[26] His throne - a cross, His crown - thorns. The High Priest detested Jesus and fiercely[27] demanded Jesus' death.

We give our Lives to God by surrendering to Him completely. He sorts problems out for us and we begin to discover Heaven while still on earth. The last two lines are a reliable guide to everyone's life. When we trust the Lord, we find Wisdom, Knowledge, Joy and are blessed by Him.

Stay with God; Love Him and serve Him - His Love will not fail us. We need not travel to find Him - He is looking for us. He is present everywhere, wherever we are.[28] For me this also means to worship in the community where I live.

3   A Morning Psalm 1

Refrain ℜ   *I lie down, sleep and I rise*
             up : the LORD takes care of me.

I have many foes
LORD : and they say, 'There is no
help for him through God.'
    You are my GLORY : in Your
    HOLINESS, LORD hear my prayer.   ℜ

I lie down and sleep :
The LORD takes care of me till
I rise up again.
    There is no need for me to
    Fear : ten thousand enemies.   ℜ

LORD arise, and help
me : there is beauty hidden
in those fighting me.
    O LORD : salvation is Your
    property,[29] we are much blest.   ℜ

This psalm is ascribed to David, written when he was fleeing from Absalom. David places the outcome into God's hands, asking that He will judge between them, and save him from his enemy if his (David's) cause is right. The fact that he was delivered on this occasion may underlie other times when innocence seems to be presumed. In Psalms 7, 17 & 26 God is being asked 'You have saved me before, am I still behaving correctly? If so please continue to help me; if not, punish me.'

There is a hint of Jesus' words in Gethsemane : '*Father not my will, but thine, be done*'.

Saint Benedict, who lived around 500 AD, established a monastic community. Each day begins eight hours after night-fall with the Night Office and this psalm is part of that Service (as is Psalm 95). St. Benedict was practical in his day and eco-friendly in hours. Seven times of daily worship are required beginning with Lauds at dawn and ending with Compline in the evening. Apart from the Night Office, silence is observed so that the first and last spoken words are said to God.

A possible step towards a prayerful life could be to learn the refrain by heart and repeat it daily on waking up. Once this is a habit the verse from Psalm 95 below comes next.[30] An excerpt from v.5a is :

> Every day allow
> the silent music[31] of GOD'S
> voice[32] to melt your heart.

4   An Evening Psalm 1
Jesus Prayer 1

Refrain ℜ   A*t night be still : look to your*
            Heart's Desire and sleep in PEACE.

God of RIGHTEOUSNESS,
be gracious to my call : and
listen to my prayer.
    Know this, the LORD shows me His
    Perfect LOVE : He hears my prayer.   ℜ

Do not go to sleep
resentful : rest in PEACE, look
to your Heart's Desire.
    When RIGHTEOUSNESS becomes your
    sacrifice : you trust the LORD.   ℜ

Chattels do not yield
enlightenment : but You LORD
fill my heart with JOY.
    I will lie down in PEACE : I
    know LORD You will keep me safe.   ℜ

This psalm is said at Compline, the last office of the day. Silence is kept until morning so that the first and last spoken words of each day are dedicated to God. If we repeat the last two lines at evening prayer or in bed, we bring this Rule into our lives.[33] There is a connection with the *Nunc Dimittis*, if we wish to 'depart in Peace'.

When pondering the events of the day, first think of the good things and thank God. They are His Gift - a sign that God loves us. This helps to keep the mind at peace during the night. After giving thanks, it is time to repent. The times when we have been discontented usually reveal where to look for faults. Unhappiness is evidence that we have thought more about ourselves than of God. When we know we have harmed another we must act - apology and reparation are called for. If this cannot be done, offer a good deed to a stranger instead.[34] Jesus speaks of the need to *'First go and make peace with your brother'* before bringing your gift to the altar (Matthew 5.23-24). St. Paul writes in Ephesians 4.26, *'If you are angry, do not let anger lead you into sin; do not let sunset find you still nursing it'.*

It is specially important to let go of anger and resentment. These both hinder sleep and actively harm our bodies. They impede the way our immune system works. It is useful to offer our other problems to God, specially when troubled by worries. This is an ideal time to use a mantra and the Jesus Prayer is particularly useful.[35] Good thoughts replace the disturbing ones. Going to sleep saying this prayer means Jesus is in our minds as the last thing before we lose consciousness.

**5   A Morning Psalm 2
Monday**

Refrain ℜ   *LORD in Your RIGHTEOUSNESS : make
plain the way that I should walk.*

LORD my God and King
consider me : I call You
and I meditate.
    I pray to you betimes : I
    look to You, I watch and wait.   ℜ

Through Your LOVE I come
to You : Your RIGHTEOUSNESS will
guide me in Your Way.
    May my words be sincere : LORD,
    set me free from wicked thoughts.   ℜ

Those who trust You give
You thanks : and those who LOVE Your
Name are blest with JOY.
    Your RIGHTEOUSNESS and GOODNESS :
    shall be their defence and shield.   ℜ

We achieve Righteousness through doing God's Will. This means allowing all His Graces to grow and flourish in our lives. I use one of the Graces each day in morning prayer, and meditate on it. This enables all the Graces to become shields.

For Saint Benedict this was the first psalm to be said on Monday morning at Lauds, the office that takes place just before dawn. The working week begins with prayer. We surrender ourselves to God's Will before doing anything else. The meaning of 'Lauds' is 'praise'. We praise God by dependence on Him. We 'look to' [36] Him to serve Him.

Although enemies of God abound, we are not perfect either. He understands us; He made us this way. I feel that He could not have created us any other way and give us independence. We are rebellious and self-centred, but we could not serve Him if we were destroyed. We can serve Him if evil within us is turned into Goodness. In order to find the Kingdom of Heaven, we need to Love our enemies and pray for them. God has plans for them too; the way we treat them may help them find it. The parable of the tares (weeds) in Matthew 13 illustrates the way God works.

Thomas Traherne gives advice on finding Joy and Heaven in this Life. Examples, from 1.28 & 29 are *'Your enjoyment of the world is never right until every morning you awake in Heaven, ... Till you can sing and rejoice in God as misers do in gold.'* H.A. Williams in *True Resurrection* writes *'Nirvana is closer to the Christian Heaven than Christians generally allow.'*

6   **Penitential Psalm 1 An Illness**
          Jesus Prayer 2

Refrain ℜ   *LORD, in Your LOVE have mercy*
                on me : heal my wounded heart.

'LORD, rebuke me not :
have mercy on my weakness,
heal my wounded heart.
    My soul is sore distressed : LORD
    in Your LOVE deliver me.   ℜ

I am close to death :
my enemies exhaust me
and I am worn out. '
    The LORD has heard my voice : my
    enemies have been turned back.   ℜ

Prayer is dialogue with God; here the human side is presented. A soul, in deep physical distress, is healed. When the psalm was written the distress felt by the writer was due to illness. He was asking God 'Why me?'[37] The weakness referred to may be in any part of our nature - body, soul or spirit. It could be emotional worries. We have been put on this world to serve God through 'creative goodness'.[38] Each of us is given a part to play in healing the sick, doing good, and binding up the broken-hearted. Tertiary Franciscans try to surrender themselves to Christ. His purpose is that they will become channels of grace and do His mighty works, including miracles.

The last two lines have a change of mood.[39] It is a positive approach to the illness. A sick person begins to feel better as soon as the illness stops getting worse. It is very important not to be impatient. The causes of the sickness – enemies – can be within, and when vanquished, they are no more. Wholeness (Holiness), if not health, will be restored. Psychology comes into recovery. Just be grateful at first, and delay an increase in activity. Never do so much in any one day that you cannot do the same and a little more the next.

When the psalm was written, illness was seen as punishment for sin. Lust, sloth and gluttony can still contribute to illness or death. Venereal disease may be an acquired infection through negligence. Less understood is that guilt damages the immune systems of a human body. Resentment, anger, and anxiety aggravate any illness. Matthew 5.22-23 says *'Make Peace with your brother (be reconciled) before offering a sacrifice to God.'* We offer our sacrifice at the Eucharist.

7   God as Judge 1

Refrain ℜ   *I trust You LORD : You LOVE the
TRUTH as well as enemies.*

LORD, my God I trust
You : save me from all those who
would devour my soul.
    If I have fostered evil :
    sentence me accordingly.   ℜ

LORD let evil fail :
for LOVE of You I would not
kill my enemy.
    The Lord helps me : He cares for
    those whose Heart's Desire is TRUTH.   ℜ

God of RIGHTEOUSNESS :
be gentle with us all when
You judge human-kind.
    I will give thanks to You : and
    praise Your Name, O God most High.   ℜ

To understand this profound psalm one needs to know that it was written by David. The immediate characters are King David and Zadok the priest (2 Samuel 15.24-27). At that time Absalom, David's son, was trying to overthrow David and kill him. David expressly ordered that Absalom should not be killed (2 Samuel 18.5).

God has plans for our enemies as well as ourselves. He loves each of them as much as he loves us. Though we may fear them, we must not kill them.

An important issue in 2013 is War. How can it be justified legally? What will be its outcome? Those defeated may have the best answers. To treat enemies gently not only shows kindness, it is Wisdom. Many of Charles Williams' novels put the last verse into perspective.

At the end of the Boer War, General Smuts, though he lost, was put in charge of South Africa. In our own times we have the example of Nelson Mandela being released from his long prison sentence and refusing to take revenge on his captors. His Truth and Reconciliation Commission worked wonders by dismantling Apartheid.

We become more involved with human-kind each time we pray this psalm meaningfully.

8   A Royal Psalm 1
God and Humankind 1

Refrain ℜ   *LORD, You have made us stewards :*
of Your works upon the earth.

LORD our Governor :
the GLORY of Your Name is
honoured everywhere.
　　You made the sun, the moon, the
　　stars : why do You visit us?   ℜ

Though made lower than
the angels : You crowned us with
GLORY and respect.
　　Yet You have given us such
　　POWER : over all Your works,   ℜ

sheep and cattle, all
wild beasts : and birds, as well as
creatures in the sea.
　　O LORD, our Governor : Your
　　Name is honoured everywhere.   ℜ

This psalm asks God *'Why do you care for human-kind?'* and the next ten psalms attempt to answer the question.

At the beginning there was nothing. God laboured when the universe was made. The physical energy of creation was immense - atomic power is evidence. The story of Creation in Genesis tells us God was tired after six days' work and rested. The outcome of this psalm is Joy after intense labour.

Mothers feel pain when giving birth; afterwards they are filled with Joy. Jesus suffered greatly as He endured the Passion. When we feel God is absent or feel pain, whether physical mental or spiritual, He is paying us the greatest compliment possible. He asks us to share in giving Eternal Life to the world. We may have to share His Cross and dereliction. We shall also share His Joy.

Artists know when their work is faulty; skilful ones turn defects into features.[40] God is the supreme artist. Our faults become assets. He wants us to share in the Joy of creation, the Joy He felt when *'He saw everything that He had made, and, behold, it was very good'.*[41] This includes animal and plant life, the physical environment,[42] in fact the whole of creation.

When we surrender ourselves to Him, the God above (Western traditions) and the divine within us (Eastern traditions) are united and The Kingdom of Heaven is created in our hearts. It is as if an electric light has been turned on - we are *'a light for all the world'.* God's Omnipotence and Royalty are returned to Him and we are lost in wonder, love and praise.

9   God and Human-kind 2
Praise for His Concern

Refrain ℜ   *I praise and thank Your Name with*
JOY O LORD : my <u>Heart's Desire</u>.

I give thanks to GOD :
I voice Your wondrous works O
LORD, my <u>Heart's Desire</u>.
    You are my JOY : Your Name and
    RIGHTEOUSNESS will never fail.   ℜ

GOD helps the oppressed :
His LOVE has never failed all
those who trust His Name.
    Pause here and meditate : His
    perfect LOVE can make you whole.   ℜ

I shall sing with JOY :
Your praises will resound from
all of Zion's gates.
    The poor will be remembered :
    meek souls will inherit earth.   ℜ

This psalm is a heartfelt song. Its writer, David, tells us that God has never failed him. He knows he is not yet out of trouble but he also knows he can rely on God in God's time.

The question asked in Psalm 8, *'Why are we here?'* begins to be resolved. We can do God's Will or follow our own, sometimes dangerous, desires. The King James version contains the word *'Higgaion'*. It is an aside and means 'stop and think what God will do to you'. I have incorporated the instruction in the words of the psalm. We can run away from God[43] or abandon ourselves to God and let Righteousness rule our Life. I prefer a positive approach.

People who dedicate their lives to Jesus Christ are the ones who consciously do His work on earth. St. Teresa of Avila wrote the well known prayer that starts, *'Christ has no body now on earth but ours ....'* It is not necessary to be a Christian to do God's works. Others are atheist or agnostic but know what is right.

Jesus cared for the poor and fatherless. The object of our existence is to put His practices into our Way of Life. Jesus is our Guide; He needs us to transmit His energy into the world.[44] To help us, God's Graces are available, through prayer, twenty-four hours a day.

Psalms 9 and 10 were written as one. The Latin numbering of the Psalms diverges here. It comes together in Psalm 147.

10   God and Human-kind 3
A Hidden God

Refrain ℜ   *O LORD, where have You gone : why*
leave us in our hour of need?

LORD, where have You gone :
Your Face stays hidden at the
time we need You most.
    The arrogant say 'Tush : there
    is no God who can stop me.'   ℜ

They wait secretly
to net the poor : and to ravish
them once they are caught.
    Arise O LORD, lift up Your
    Hand : do not forget the poor.   ℜ

Heathen influence
has been transformed : LORD You will
rule for evermore.
    You save the humble from their
    fears[45] : and help the fatherless.   ℜ

How long shall we have to wait for God to act? We do not know. That He does act is seen in the final verse. While we wait we can ponder this: 'How long will He wait before we respond to His wishes for us?'

God pays us a compliment and asks us to trust Him as John's Gospel tells us that Jesus trusted the Father. He honours us but we feel hurt because we don't see immediate results. We do not see evidence of God's Wisdom, or even think He knows a better way.

Aung San Suu Kyi thought it better to endure pain because she was doing what is right.[46] I believe we should surrender pain to God, asking Him to use it to reduce suffering somewhere in the world. One idea is to practise it in small ways. We offer every disaster or mishap, illness or pain, major or minor, to God. We ask Him to use this, somehow, to help someone, somewhere.

The opposite helps too. To ask God to guide us at each stage of projects we believe we are doing for Him. Our idea may not be the best. Allow Him to show us the scheme that is perfect, both for us and all human-kind. We will then see this happening before our eyes.

We all are flawed; by Loving those we do not understand, we create empathy. To give the benefit of the doubt may cost us dear. It was the same for Jesus. He experienced dreadful pain at the hands of human beings who behaved like animals. Judas handed Him over to the Romans thinking it would help Jesus' cause. I know that Judas would have been forgiven had he returned instead of hanging himself.

11   Confidence in God 1
His Righteousness

Refrain ℜ   *I trust the LORD to shelter*
me : His LOVE is RIGHTEOUSNESS.

I trust in the LORD :
'How dare you say "Fly like a
bird to mountain-tops"?
    Ungodly folk will ambush those :
    whose <u>Heart's Desire</u> is TRUTH.   ℜ

If they undermine
Your GOODNESS : can you learn the
Way to RIGHTEOUSNESS?
    In HOLINESS, from heav'n : the
    LORD desires to help the poor.   ℜ

He is looking at
the human-race : with eyes that
value RIGHTEOUSNESS.
    Our evil is transformed : *with*
    inextinguishable Blaze.[47]   ℜ

Perfect RIGHTEOUSNESS
belongs to GOD : this is His
LOVE above all else.
    All upright souls receive the
    right : to gaze upon His Face.[48]   ℜ

In this psalm the writer faces those who question his reasons for turning to God with confidence. Psalm 121 offers a helpful insight. When you get to the mountain top the view is so fantastic that you can be counselled by the quiet serenity of the mountain itself.

The Psalmist has a firm faith. He allows God's Graces to grow within himself through meditation and contemplation. T.N. Hanh writes *'In each of us is the seed of understanding. That seed is God. It is also the Buddha. If you doubt the existence of that seed of understanding, you doubt God and you doubt the Buddha'.*[49] When we actively seek Righteousness (acting in accord with God's will) in Buddhist terms we are mindful of Him. Where mindfulness is present so is Love.[50]

The experience of God gazing on the human race, and our gazing upon His Face in return, is what we aim for in contemplation. However, it can overwhelm us. St. Teresa of Avila, St. Francis, St. Clare and others had such experiences.

There are imperfections within each one of us. When pondering on this psalm I like to bear in mind that I am the one needing treatment. Isaiah was purified by live coals on his lips, but was able to respond *'Here am I, send me'.*[51] We know God is Love, not destruction. He is like a surgeon who uses an anaesthetic when cauterising a wound.

12   Confidence in God 2
His Purity

Refrain ℜ *God's words are unalloyed : like*
silver seven times refined.

    Lord deliver me :
for those who vow to serve You
all their LIFE are few.
    Transform all lying lips : and
    use their words to do Your Will.   ℜ

I will act says GOD :
give POWER to the meek and
safety to the poor.
    GOD'S words are unalloyed : like
    silver seven times refined.   ℜ

Wicked men abound :
they flaunt themselves, their love of
evil grows and grows.
    LORD, be our safeguard, and
    preserve us : enemies abound.   ℜ

'Purified seven times in the fire' reminds us of fire and brimstone. I prefer a more constructive approach.
- The disciples who walked to Emmaus felt their hearts burning.
- At Pentecost God's fire filled the disciples with His Spirit, but did not burn them. In modern language they were 'fired up'.
- When we have been provoked our tempers may blaze with anger as we try to purify someone else. Later, when we ponder the events, we may think of ways to react in a more kindly way in future.

The Letter of Saint James reminds us that human tongues can burn others. It is easy to see the faults in other people and we witness endless criticism of individuals in today's media. Rather than passing critical comment, we can pray for people. In talking to and about others, we should aim to be discreet, discerning, and sincere, then our tongues will 'win the day'.

God's message to us is one of Love. When guided by the Spirit and its fruits, we can be members of God's surgical team.

We do God's work when we show unconditional Love for friend or enemy. By Loving those we find difficult we begin to understand them, forgive their failings[52] and cease to fear them.

Those who reject God may begin to respect Him when they see concord between different denominations and faiths. God loves all people - Christian or not.

13   Surrender to God's Providence

Refrain ℜ   *I trust You LORD : Your LOVE saved*
me, and I am filled with JOY.

LORD, how long, how long,
how long, how long : shall my foes
triumph over me?
 Enlighten me O LORD : or
 I may fall asleep and die.   ℜ

LORD, I trust Your LOVE
to thwart my enemies : and
give me JOY when free.
 I shall tell out Your Name : You
 granted me my <u>Heart's Desire</u>.   ℜ

The fourfold cry *'How long?'* expresses the human frustration at the apparent slowness of God to relieve our distress. This was a difficulty thousands of years ago, just as much as it is today.

Jesus, when on the cross, seemed to plead with the Father – *'Why have you forsaken me?'* We know these words come from Psalm 22. This was when He was at His most creative - He was giving us Life through His death. Like Psalm 22, this psalm ends with a joyful note. Human mothers have always had similar feelings when giving birth. The ultimate effect in each case is Joy.

There is a complementary thought. What does God feel about us? *'How long will you take to accept and carry out the responsibility I have given to you to care for the world?'*

God's Goodness is not completely revealed to us until we take our full part in His creation. Finding ways we can contribute to life on earth is part of our purpose.

We also need to be aware of, and to celebrate, our freedom with a party. The Eucharist provides an opportunity to give that communal act of thanks.

14   **God and Human Kind 4**
          God's Thoughts

Refrain ℜ   *O LORD : my* <u>*Heart's Desire*</u> *is*
             WISDOM, JOY, and RIGHTEOUSNESS.

'God does not exist'
say fools : they think that GOODNESS
is not their concern.
 The LORD reviews mankind : for
 souls with WISDOM who seek God. ℜ

His desire is TRUTH
JOY, PEACE, respect : and KNOWLEDGE
of His RIGHTEOUSNESS.
 These Graces are possessed by
 humble souls : but they are scorned. ℜ

Is there anyone
in Zion : who has POWER
to save Israel?
 When GOD has set His people
 free : we shall be filled with JOY. ℜ

The differences between this psalm and number 53 are small but significant. Here the word used for God is Jehovah. In Psalm 53 the Gentiles, with many gods, are addressed.

The fool of v.1, in the Old Testament, saw God as of no account. Julia Neuberger writes of the medieval custom[53] of ethical wills. Parents wrote these for their children, summing up the best advice they had learned, a legacy of Wisdom. They regarded Wisdom as important a legacy as material possessions.

The refrain for the psalm reminds us of the status we seek. When Our Father's Desire is the same as our own, we will succeed. He may not do what we expect; our will therefore has to be flexible. The *'poor in spirit'* of the Sermon on the Mount understand this. They know they may be mocked because they believe and say *'Jesus is Lord'*. They *'know their need of God'*. They trust Him[54] and are at Peace. They are not over-busy with worldly concerns, or consumed by desire for *'vanity'* at someone else's expense.

Another way to look at the situation is to remember that God planted the seeds of His Graces in our souls at conception. Here He is considering how well those seeds have grown. No human being is perfect. We have all failed, in New Testament terms, to come up to the mark - or to hit the bulls-eye. We believe that God, in His Infinite Wisdom, sent His Son Jesus Christ, to come from Zion to redeem us through His death.

15   Another Ten Commandments

Refrain ℜ *LORD, who may live with You? Souls*
whose LOVE is Your HOLINESS.

LORD who will abide
with You : or rest upon Your
Hill of HOLINESS?
    A sincere heart, who speaks the
    TRUTH : and shows Your RIGHTEOUSNESS. ℜ

Speaks with courtesy,
gives generously : and sits down
in the lowest place;
    she helps those who have faith : and
    keeps her word at any cost.   ℜ

She will freely[55] lend
her money : she will not be
bribed to harm the poor.
    Each soul that does all of these
    things : will always live in PEACE.   ℜ

This is a psalm that was sung by pilgrims waiting outside the Temple. Each commandment was sung by a cantor. The people answered. Responsorial Psalms are based on this tradition.

This psalm is social in its requirements and it still applies. Those outside the Church expect sincerity of its members. If lax conduct is seen in a Christian, that person's religion will be questioned. Holiness for non-believers means integrity. For a believer it has another dimension - Love - and it is expected of all who seek the Kingdom of God. It is not mentioned but is hidden behind every line of the psalm. Jesus expects His followers to show Love to everyone, whether friend or foe.

Human beings respond more happily to praise than criticism. Praise what you can, and pray for what is bad. John 2.25 reminds us that Jesus did not need evidence about *'any man'*. He knew what was in their hearts and was generous with Compassion.

Many of us have hunches about the thoughts of others. When speaking our truth from the heart, great caution must be exercised. Knowledge of the person you are dealing with matters. Not everyone can bear this truth about themselves, especially someone who is depressed or who feels guilty. Self-esteem may be damaged and hopelessness exacerbated.

Kindness is always the best course of expression and action.

16   The Source of True Happiness

Refrain ℜ   *I trust You LORD : my refuge*
and the source of all my JOY.

LORD I trust in You :
You are my refuge and the
source of all my JOY.
    LORD You supply my needs : and
    choose the Cup that's best for me.   ℜ

Beauteous is the land :
a heritage of GOODNESS
is marked out for me.
    I thank the LORD who counsels
    me : with WISDOM in the night.   ℜ

I keep Him in mind :
with Him as my defence I
know I cannot fall.
    He fills my heart with JOY : He
    is my GLORY and my hope.   ℜ

Death will not prevail
against my soul : You will show
me the path of LIFE.
    It leads to You : the source of
    perfect JOY for evermore.   ℜ

Psalms 15-18 make an interesting sequence. This psalm develops the last verse of Psalm 15. We are dependent on God. He provides us with food for body, mind and spirit - our *'daily (Celestial) bread'* and with *'every kind of excellence and Peace'*.[56]

J.P. de Caussade explores these thoughts. Everything that happens to us is part of the counsel that God gives us. Goodness is hidden there but we may not be able to see it. Surrender to God's Will at times of distress or illness makes manifest His great Love for us. We are not always aware of His support. Old time obstetricians had a phrase *'masterly inactivity'*. They did nothing, comforted their patient, and let nature work things out, only interfering if absolutely necessary.

H.A Williams[57] encourages us to create Heaven on earth otherwise we might not know it even if we were there! When God and His attributes are missing it is easier for alcohol, drugs, sex, violence or other temptations to take His place.

Substance abuse 'users' spend their time looking for their next 'fix'. They do not appreciate healthy food, exercise or beauty. Between addicts and others there is a mental barrier which is hard to cross. It resembles the gulf in Jesus' parable of the rich man and the beggar, Lazarus. If addicts are to be helped, trust has to be established. Addicts need to feel valued as individuals - this helps both the detox and rehabilitation stages. Alcoholics Anonymous does this through its programmes. Both church members and drug users live in the same world, both are valued by God.

17   An Appeal to God for Justice and Grace

Refrain ℜ   *Lord, Save my Soul : that I may*
                    see the GLORY of Your Face.

LORD of RIGHTEOUSNESS
consider well my cause : and
plea of innocence.
     Your verdict will acquit me :
     for your eyes discern the TRUTH.   ℜ

You have tested me
by night : and know that all my
Heart's Desires are pure.
     Support me as I tread the
     path You choose : in case I slip.   ℜ

Show Your Perfect LOVE
to me : for You save those who
put their trust in You.
     LORD, may Your wings protect me :
     as the apple of Your eye.   ℜ

Enemies abound :
they hide to catch me and to
take away my Soul.
     Deliver me : that I may
     see the GLORY of Your Face.   ℜ

The Psalmist knows he has done his best. He knows that God's Love is *marvellous* and that it will make allowances for failure.

The self-confidence of the references to good behaviour might seem overbearing. The Psalmist knows he needs God's help to live a life that is in keeping with His will. The Gelineau translation makes clear that a court scene is envisaged, a sentence is about to be passed. It helps if we see the words as a plea of 'not guilty' in a court of law. The writer has been presenting the best case possible to avoid being condemned to eternal damnation. He hopes the judgement will be in his favour.

'Lord, may Your wings protect me as the apple of Your eye' is said each night at Compline. It is a good one to say in evening prayers or once in bed, before going to sleep. It strikes a happy note.

The last verse is a good one to contemplate as well and offers Eternal Life as a possibility. If we think about how we can, in our own way, take part in *'True Resurrection'* this could be an excellent resolution for the next day.

Refrains   ℜ 1   *Each time I pray : God's POWER will*
                        save me from my enemies.
             ℜ 2   *You give my darkness Light : my*
                        feet will reach the mountain tops.

LORD You are my LOVE :
Your POWER is my defence and
gives me HOLINESS.
    When fear of death surrounded
    me : the LORD delivered me.   ℜ 1

He rewarded me
for RIGHTEOUSNESS : He saved me
when I was distressed.
    O LORD you give my darkness
    light : I will scale every wall.   ℜ 2

God's Way is sincere :
His POWER keeps me safe in
every step I take.
    He gives me feet like those of
    deer : I reach the mountain-tops.   ℜ 2

God is LIFE and POWER :
He has delivered me from
cruel enemies.
    I praise His Name and tell the
    world : His LOVE will never end.   ℜ 2

This psalm is wonderful to read when we have reason for thanksgiving.

The song comes in 2 Samuel 22. It is David's thanksgiving for delivery from Saul and the problems that followed his death. David knows he would have failed without God's Power.

In the Lord's Prayer when we say *'deliver us from evil'* we could think *'I cannot do this on my own.'* In private prayer, I follow the words *'Lead us not into temptation'* with *'Be with us when our faith is put to the test*[58] *and deliver us from evil.'* Jesus, who taught us the Prayer, was put to the test. He also supports us in the *'valley of the shadow of death'* when we face trials of our own.

Human relationships can be similarly supportive. We achieve more when surrounded by people who have the same intent. This support can be witnessed in prayer groups and in happy families. The members radiate Love to everyone they meet and *'etch happy memories on many hearts'*.[59]

Couples work well when they work with each person's strengths. One may have an idea and the other know how to achieve it. A Christian married couple will have the added support of knowing they can call on the healing power of God when they face challenges. I believe that people in all partnerships are blessed by God (whether they recognise Him or not) and can ask God for healing.

It is interesting to note that the words *healing, holiness* and *wholeness* all have the same derivation.

19   The Designer of the Universe

Refrain ℜ   *We see God's GLORY in the*
heav'ns : He gives us LIFE and JOY.

God reveals Himself :
the GLORY of the skies show
His Creative POWER.
  With Silent Music[60] : KNOWLEDGE
  is passed on by Day and Night.   ℜ

Every land on earth
will see the radiant sun rise
up : to give us light.
  GOD'S Word is pure : it gives new
  LIFE, and WISDOM to the meek.   ℜ

His decrees give JOY :
they are worth more than gold and
yield a great reward.
  Reveal to me O LORD : the
  faults I would forgive myself.   ℜ

LORD, guard me from pride :
may I serve those I meet in
true humility.
  To tell about Your POWER and
  serve You : is my Heart's Desire.   ℜ

The psalm reminds us of evidence for God's existence. The Glory and Beauty of the universe are revealed. The light from the sun's energy gives Life to the earth. Enlightenment from God is the energy that feeds the spirit.

In the second stanza I have used *'Word'* instead of *'law'* to link Old and New Testaments. Our bodies, minds and spirits are subject to Natural Laws, as are all other forms of animal and vegetable life. Natural laws paint on a wide canvas and, in my opinion, show that Christianity and science are compatible. Scientists discover how the laws work, theologians explore why. The two groups do not compete.

Meditation on the Glory of heaven and earth, whether through being in nature or experiencing it through the lens of art or music, can bring us great Joy. When we listen to God's Silent Music through Contemplative Prayer, we tune into His Will and His Grace and we acquire Knowledge of the reason for our creation. The Gospel of John says we *'worship Him in Spirit and in TRUTH'*.[61]

The references to faults (sin) foreshadow the way the New Testament presents them. They have a wider meaning than to break God's commands, as is mentioned in references to the Jesus Prayer in the introduction and Psalm 51. Our failings can cause us great anxiety if we do not remind ourselves of God's infinite mercy and His understanding of our weaknesses.

20   A Royal Psalm 2
Prayer for the King before Battle

Refrain ℜ   *The Name of God the LORD : will*
                      keep you safe when in distress.

May the LORD hear you :
and through His Name protect you
when you are distressed.
    His HOLINESS will give you
    POWER : through Your Sacrifice.　　　ℜ

When your Heart's Desire
maintains His Will : He will grant
you your every wish.
    We shall be filled with JOY : the
    Name of GOD will save us all.　　　ℜ

I know God the LORD,
with His right hand : will cover
His Anointed One.
    His HOLINESS, His Name and
    POWER : save those who trust in Him.　　ℜ

The words are the prayers of the king's subjects on his behalf in the coming battle. God is asked to give their king Power to achieve victory. Their lives depend on the outcome. They will probably be killed if he is defeated.

Success in a venture is always more likely if there is a positive attitude before action is taken. This psalm is one of trust in the Lord. Psalm 21 shows that the request was granted.

Heart's Desire is a key phrase. When this is in accord with God's will for us, our wishes will be granted. We shall find Joy. Miracles occur. I believe this is one of the reasons for our creation. Other people notice the Joy, even if they do not know its source - our union with God in Christ.

We discover we are carried through life's difficult times. There will be times of pain, illness, and disappointment. Richard Rhor in *Falling Upwards*[62] regards these as essential for our development. Only when we can forgive ourselves for our own failings, can we begin to forgive others. Then we can rejoice, understand, smile, and be generous to all.

The sacrifice referred to in the psalm is one that would advance David's cause. 3000 years later we have a different King. His crown was of thorns, His Sacrifice was His own Life, His victory was over death.

In our busy lives, is our faith in Jesus' victory one of our priorities? Do possessions take precedence? Is our faith put in mechanical chariots? Do we celebrate Eastertide as a time of great Joy - even greater than Christmas?

21   **A Royal Psalm 3**
       Gratitude for Victory

Refrain ℜ   *Your saving POWER and JOY have*
             giv'n Your King : His <u>Heart's Desire</u>.

LORD of POWER and JOY :
You Saved our King and granted
Him his <u>Heart's Desire.</u>
   Your GOODNESS Blessed Him, Gold has
   crowned him : You renewed His LIFE.   ℜ

You gave him renown
with GLORY : and the JOY of
gazing on Your face.
   He trusted You O Lord : and
   through Your LOVE all will be well.   ℜ

Your right hand will find
His enemies : its heat will
change their evil ways.
   O LORD we offer songs of
   Praise : in honour of Your POWER.   ℜ

The victory prayed for in the last psalm has been granted. The king's subjects express their delight, giving thanks to God for the strength of their leader. He has his Heart's Desire – victory.

Orthodox weddings use this psalm and Psalm 8. The couple are treated royally. They are crowned; they drink from a common cup which has been blessed; they celebrate the Eucharist and the creativity of Divine Love which we share.[63] They are given their Heart's Desire - each other - and the ability to pro-create new life on God's behalf. Coptic weddings are even more sensual.

This is another psalm with some words we find difficult to accept. The last stanza needs consideration so that a Christian meaning can be found - 'the heat' of transformation.

Elsewhere in the Bible fire originating from the Lord brings benefits. To beat swords into plough-shares and spears into pruning-hooks, as in Isaiah 2.4, would require heat. Much energy is needed before weapons of war can be turned to tools for Peace.

Human transformation took place when the fire of the Spirit settled on the apostles and a bright light converted Saul into Paul. In all these things God acts through Jesus' atonement, or as I was taught, 'a†-one-ment', for the human race.

22   Why Have You Forsaken Me?

Refrain ℜ   *My God, my God hear me : O*
why have You forsaken me?

O my God, my God,
consider me : O why have
You forsaken me?
   O God, pay heed, my prayers are
   Spurned : at night I find no PEACE.   ℜ
God of HOLINESS :
our line was not confounded
by its trust in You.
   Of me men say : He trusted
   God, let God deliver Him.   ℜ
You are He who drew
me from the womb : from then on
You have been my God.
   Men pierced my hands and feet : LORD
   save my darling from the dog.   ℜ
LORD you rescued me :
when unicorns surrounded
me, You heard my prayer.
   I will tell out and praise Your
   Name : to everyone I meet.   ℜ
He shall feed the poor :
all nations and all people
shall turn to the LORD.
   I shall tell those yet to be
   born : The LORD accomplished it.   ℜ

These are some of my favourite thoughts about this psalm :

1. As we know from Genesis 1.2, God is at His most creative when He starts with nothing. Jesus had nothing. He was scorned and His Life was taken from Him. He gave us Eternal Life as a result and transformed evil into Goodness for ever. We worship Him and encourage our children to do so to ensure future generations will be aware of His Righteousness.

2. Jesus said the whole of this psalm on the Cross. He knew its triumphant ending. The last single word in Hebrew is *'The Lord has done this'* or *'It is finished'*.

3. Thomas Traherne sees only good in this psalm[64] and ignores the difficult verses at the beginning. I see a link with the Magnificat where similar thoughts foretell Jesus' future.

4. Mary said the Magnificat at the beginning of Jesus' life and we are reminded in this psalm that she was at the foot of the cross. Pergolesi's *Stabat Mater* is a duet between female voices. They slide from harmony to dissonance and back in an agonising way that convey her feelings.

5. I was taught Divinity by Eric Milner-White who said the *Te Deum* should end *'I shall never be confounded'* not *'May I never be confounded'*. The words are the same in Greek.

6. Perhaps the Centurion whose servant was healed by Jesus was the one who oversaw the Crucifixion. If so the words *'truly this was a Son of God'* have a greater meaning.

7. We add our redemptive efforts to His if we accept unmerited suffering without complaint[65] - not easy.

8. Where are you in this scene? I know where I would like to be but wonder if I would have the courage.

- Am I among the crowd looking on?
- Have I fled away? Pergolesi's music would encourage me, out of Love for Jesus, to stay at the foot of the cross.

23   The Good Shepherd -
How God Cares for Us

Refrain ℜ   *The LORD will shepherd me : and*
there is nothing I shall lack.

GOD will shepherd me :
and He ensures that there is
nothing I shall lack.
    He feeds me in green pasture :
    close to streams that quench my thirst.   ℜ

He renews my LIFE
by paths of RIGHTEOUSNESS : e'en
for His Own Name's sake.
    I shall not fear the vale of
    death : for You are there with me.   ℜ

You give me a feast
my foes can see : anoint my
head, and fill my Cup.
    Your GOODNESS and unfailing
    LOVE : are with me evermore.   ℜ

The opening shows us that the Lord, as our shepherd, will always cherish us. Sheep readily follow their leader. This is noticeable in particular with lambs that have been hand reared. They follow their shepherd hoping to obtain another meal even if they have only just had one. So a flock which knows its shepherd is sure that it will be guided to green pastures and fresh water.

Jewish tradition relates the psalm to the time when Saul, as King, was seeking to kill David. Having been a shepherd, David was well equipped to be a king. Both roles call for leadership qualities.

'He renews my LIFE' [66] reminds us that, as our faith grows, we must move to pastures new. The Lord, who shepherds us, will be our guide. Sheep do not follow a 'hireling' and the thought of Jesus as the Good Shepherd is inescapable. It is seen in Psalm 119.176 - a plea from a lost sheep to the shepherd to come and find him.

The words *'valley of the shadow of death'* are not in most versions; *'glen of gloom'* and *'deepest darkness'* are found elsewhere. They recall Gethsemane as a place where Jesus has already been. Saint John of the Cross spoke of the *'dark night of the soul'*. In both places Jesus will support [67] us, if we ask.

Happier thoughts come with the list of ways that God helps us: protection from enemies, the oil of healing [68] and the Eucharistic cup of wine. Emphasis is put on the abundance of God's unconditional love for us and the nature of that love. We don't have to prove ourselves worthy. We are. Our enemies can see and come to share the feast. They only have to ask.

Refrain ℜ   *GOD blesses souls whose hearts are*
Pure : and live in RIGHTEOUSNESS.

Earth belongs to GOD :
with all it's GOODNESS, and each
LIFE that is therein.
    Who may ascend His Hill of
    HOLINESS : and stand thereon?   ℜ

Souls whose hands are clean
and hearts are pure : treat neighbours
well and are sincere.
    The LORD will bless and save : all
    souls that live in RIGHTEOUSNESS.   ℜ

Gates and Ancient doors
make way : allow the King of
Glory to come in.
    What King : the King of POWER
    GLORY, our Eternal God.   ℜ

The psalm was used was at dedication festivals, when pilgrims arrived at the Temple. The doors would have been shut, and those outside shouted 'Open up'. The reply would have been 'Why?' They were told in no uncertain terms. The ceremony was re-enacting the time when David returned to Jerusalem with the Ark of the Lord . The first two lines recall the first chapter of Genesis.

The psalm would be a very good one to use at a stewardship service. I have transcribed 'fullness' into 'Goodness'. This stresses Traherne's Comments in Century 3.74. *'We are made in the Image of God'.* We should value earth's treasures - its constituents and living-beings - as much as He does.

Jesus in the Gospel of Saint John, chapter 17, asks us to believe in Him and to say so. He and the Father are one; both come and dwell within us. We then have blessings without number, Peace and Righteousness among them. Each of these has hazards. In Luke and John we are told that the Peace may not be comfortable - in the modern sense of the word. Jesus fulfilled the Righteousness of God, as He predicted at His Baptism according to Saint Matthew. The *'Glory of God in the Highest'* gives Peace on earth for souls whose hands and hearts are pure, and who do His will as Saint John writes in his First epistle. People other than Christians who do His will, without being aware of it, are included.

Holman Hunt's picture *'The Light of the World'* is an allegory. There is no handle on the door. Jesus can only knock on the outside, asking us to open it so that He may enter into our lives. He can only do so with our permission.

25   Protection and Forgiveness
Jesus Prayer 2

Refrain ℜ   *Forgive my grievous Sin O*
LORD : and grant me days of JOY.

LORD, my <u>Heart's Desire</u>,
give me support : for I have
put my trust in You.
    My enemies attack : but
    those who Hope in You will win.   ℜ

LORD show me Your Way,
teach me Your TRUTH : You are my
Saviour and my God.
    Do not recall my failures :
    show me GOODNESS and Your LOVE.   ℜ

LORD for Your Name's sake
forgive my grievous guilt : and
grant me days of JOY.
    Guide gentle souls along Your
    Way : it leads to RIGHTEOUSNESS.   ℜ

In Hebrew this psalm is an alphabetical one, with four repeated themes:

1. I hope and trust in the Lord
2. I look to the Lord
3. I have sinned
4. His love saves me from my sins.

The Psalmist feels inadequate, as we all do at times when we think of God. We can all relate to the sense of being overwhelmed by *'enemies'*. The writer asks God to take the initiative and he thereby gives Omnipotence, God's Power, back to Him. There will be success, though not always along the path we would choose.

For us this is an Advent psalm, without reference to Death and Judgement. The presentation is more like Part 1 of Handel's Messiah, making a highway through the desert.

The theme of Love is an important one. It is parental. Provided we are humble enough, we are guided through our lives by a Father who loves us, created and forgives us. He has a maternal concern for us too.[69] This dual concept of God is a major factor in *'The Shack'* by William Young.

The experience of being loved, in turn, allows us to be generous. Traherne writes in *'Centuries'*, *'God, by satisfying my self-love, hath enabled and engaged me to love others.'*

26   A Sincere Man Faces Judgement

Refrain ℜ   *Lord be my judge : I trust that*
You will find me innocent.

Vindicate me LORD :
I trust You will pronounce that
I am innocent.
    Test out my Heart's Desire : Your
    LOVE and TRUTH will be my guide.   ℜ

I shall wash my hands
in innocence : and worship
at your altar LORD.
    I shall sing songs of praise : and
    thank You for Your miracles.   ℜ

LORD, I LOVE Your house :
its beauty, and the GLORY
of Your dwelling place.
    LORD in Your LOVE deliver
    Me : to walk in innocence.   ℜ

This psalm contains three features:

1. Judgement
2. Innocence
3. Thanksgiving.

1. The writer of the psalm appeals to God as if in a Court of Justice. He feels threatened by people hostile to God. They offer to bribe him with gold in the Gelineau version of this psalm.

2. He believes himself innocent, he has not accepted bribes. I have chosen the word 'sincere' in the title. It comes from the Latin meaning 'without wax', we would say 'unvarnished'.

The writer knows he is not perfect. All that he 'owns' is lent to him by God and all that he can offer is his heart. He is happiest when in God's House, and God's Glory is at hand.

3. Thanksgiving is another name for the Eucharist. Christians believe that the elements being consecrated are unblemished. The priest washes his hands before the Offertory Prayer in the same way that a cook washes his hands so that his own lack of health is not passed on to us. Our spirituality is then nourished by healthy food.

27   Confidence in God

Refrain ℜ :   *Look to the LORD : for He is*
                coming very close to you.

My salvation, light,
and LIFE is GOD : of whom then
shall I be afraid?
    An army may besiege me :
    I shall still be confident.   ℜ

One thing that I ask
of Him : to gaze upon His
beauty evermore.
    When troubled He will keep me
    safe : within His HOLINESS.   ℜ

Though my mother and
my father will leave me : the
LORD'S LOVE never fails.
    Teach me the Way to walk : and
    keep me safe from enemies.   ℜ

I know I shall see
the GOODNESS of the LORD : and
find Eternal LIFE.
    Look to the LORD, seize POWER, take
    heart : and wait upon the LORD.   ℜ

I like to think that when Moses gazed upon Yahweh, He gazed back. Moses' face was so radiant that he had to veil his face when he returned from the mountain. There is a legend about Saint Francis and Saint Clare at prayer together. Their faces became so bright at one time that the area was lit up. People thought there was a fire.

The phrase *'Look to'* is found in Psalm 123. This is also a command for bell-ringers - the ringer of the treble bell tells others to *'look to'* their neighbour when starting a peal.

Servants *'look unto their master's hand'* [70] for orders. For Christians Our Lord and Master who commands us is Jesus Christ. We *'look to'* Him. We are also asked to *'wait'* upon the Lord, either to serve as waiter, or to *'be patient'*.

Faith is a key to this psalm. The threefold reference to 'heart' in the Book of Common Prayer means that a heartfelt faith allows God to influence our lives on earth. His care for us is greater than that of our fathers and mothers, who leave us. When we aim to serve the Lord, He gives us the Power needed to complete our part in it.

What does *'the land of the living'* mean? For me it is Eternal Life, or 'people who are aware of God' in a manner that is meaningful to them. Souls can *'be still and know that I AM GOD'* [71] in many ways. Buddhists attain 'enlightenment', Hindus aim for Nirvana and the Tao (the Way) is another. The first of the three Tertiary Franciscan ways of service is 'to live in an atmosphere of praise and prayer'. Christ says *'I AM the Way, the Truth and the Life'*. Eastern and Christian beliefs interlock.

28   A Plea for Help - Thanksgiving when it Arrives

Refrain ℜ1   *O Lord, my Rock of POWER :*
                       hear my cry or I shall die.

Refrain ℜ2   *You are the shepherd of Your*
                       people : feed them evermore.

LORD, consider me :
You are my Rock of POWER,
hear me or I die.
    I humbly pray to You : O
    LORD of LOVE and HOLINESS.   ℜ1

Help me be sincere
in heart : each time I speak of
PEACE with those I meet.
    Support souls who have broken
    down : to build things up again.   ℜ1

Bless-ed be the LORD :
For He has heard the humble
prayers I made to Him.
    He is my Heart's Desire : I
    trusted Him, I shall be safe.   ℜ2

I shall dance for JOY :
the LORD'S Anointed One will
shield me with His POWER.
    LORD, bless Your people, be their
    Shepherd : feed them evermore.   ℜ2

This psalm, like many others, begins with deep despair, illness, physical illness, or anxiety. The exact problem is not clear. Because of the reference to God as a Rock, I like to think of the situation in 1 Samuel 20. Here David hides behind a rock. It enables Jonathan to convey a coded message to David about Saul. Saul was feeling insulted by David's behaviour, and seeks to kill him. David is in a dilemma. He cannot go back; he would like to 'sort out' Saul but does not. Saul is God's anointed King. Instead, David is fed on consecrated bread - 1 Samuel 21.5. He does not kill Saul when he has the opportunity - 1 Samuel 24.6 and 26.11.

There are other special Rocks in the Bible. The one struck by Moses to yield water - Exodus 17.6; the house built on rock in Matthew 7.24-25 and *'You are Peter ... and upon this Rock I shall build my Church'*. The profession is found in all Gospels though these particular words are from Matthew 16.15 & 18.

We, like David, have dilemmas. When they arise, we can seek counsel from those who dedicate their lives to God's Name. We may consume His sacred food and look to God's Graces, especially Love, to shield us.

For us, new opportunities arise after sacramental confession and recovery from illness. Subsequently we may feel called to act, even if only on a small scale, to save, help, feed and elevate the spirits of God's people everywhere.

29   **Our Omnipotent and Omnipresent God**

Refrain ℜ   *The LORD is King, we praise His*
                 Name : His blessing is His PEACE.

Recognise the LORD :
He rules the Universe in
GLORY and in POWER.
    Give honour to His Name : and
    worship Him in HOLINESS.   ℜ

His voice Rules the sea :
the thunder of His voice will
shatter cedar trees.
    His voice, with forks of lightning :
    makes the mountains skip like calves.   ℜ

His voice makes the hinds
give birth to young : His voice will
strip the forest bare.
    Our King will give His people
    POWER : and bless them with PEACE.   ℜ

This is one of the earliest psalms, and may once have praised Ba'al. It stresses God's control of nature in the picturesque language of the Ugarit people who lived in Lebanon and Syria. They worshipped Ba'al and used human sacrifice, an act deplored by the Hebrews. The process shows how ideas from earlier religions become incorporated into later ones. (The same method was used to introduce Christianity to indigenous cultures in this country.)

The psalm was once used to celebrate Israel's Autumn Festival. At this time of year the rains bring fertility to the soil in a dramatic manner. God blesses them.

The phrase *'The voice of the Lord'* is used seven times in some translations. Seven is a divine number and stresses the significance of giving Him worship on earth as well as in heaven.

If we interpret the Lord's *'Voice'* as His *'Word'* (John 1.1-14) this psalm foreshadows the Incarnation. Life, Light, Power and Glory all appear in the New Testament passage. For good measure Angels sing of Glory and Peace at Jesus' birth.

Refrain ℟   *O LORD my God, I called to*
               You : and You have made me whole.

I will praise You LORD :
I called, You made me whole and
brought me back to LIFE.
        Remember Him, souls who LOVE
        Him : think on His HOLINESS.   ℟

He LOVES LIFE, not wrath :
dark nights for souls will pass, and
JOY will come with dawn.
        Prosperity brought pleasure :
        God's great GOODNESS set me up.   ℟

Then my troubles came :
I humbly asked the LORD for
mercy and for help.
        You turned my mourning into
        dance : and You clothed me with JOY. ℟

I shall always sing
Your praise within my soul : no
one shall silence me.
        O LORD my God, I shall thank
        You : for all eternity.   ℟

This psalm was sung at the re-dedication of the Temple in 515 BC and again in 164 BC.[72]

There is Joy in the Psalmist's heart. He had been severely troubled by an illness. In deep humility he asked God for healing and for help.

The Gospels show us how deeply Jesus loved people. He knew their troubles and was able to tease out their problems with surgical precision. The person concerned could respond as seemed fit. The self-esteem of the Samaritan woman by the well in John 4.5-42 was left intact. She immediately became a witness for Christ.

As Christians we continue the work of helping others wherever we can. However, when we encounter depressed people, we can find it hard to know what to say. They are engulfed by what St. John of the Cross called '*the dark night of the soul'*. '*Pull yourself together'* is harmful - if they knew how to do so, they would. Empathy with their problems is the answer but this requires expertise. Samaritans are trained befrienders. We, too, can listen with empathy, feeling Love for them deep inside our hearts, without giving advice. This goes a long way.

> This Prayer makes a useful variant to the Jesus Prayer :
> Lord Jesus Christ, the Son of God :
> have mercy on me, make me whole
> And bring me back to Life again.

31 Patterns of Illness 2
Evening Psalm 2

Refrain ℜ   *LORD You reserve great GOODNESS :*
for all souls who trust in You.

LORD my mind is clear :
I trust Your RIGHTEOUSNESS, it
will deliver me.
    Incline Your ear to me : and
    for Your Name's sake keep me safe.   ℜ

I commend myself
into Your hands : for You have
saved me, GOD of TRUTH.
    My JOY is Your unfailing
    LOVE : and gift of Liberty.   ℜ

When I am downcast,
in body or in mind : be
gracious to me LORD.
    My sin has caused disease : and
    I am loathsome to my friends.   ℜ

Smile on me with LOVE,
and plenteous GOODNESS : I will
thank You evermore.
    Be strong and trust the LORD : He
    will give you your Heart's Desire.   ℜ

This is another psalm for healing. The nature of the condition is not known but loathsome skin diseases were regarded as leprosy. The Psalmist would have been treated as a leper.

This is also one of the psalms St. Benedict prescribed for use at Compline - the office at the end of day. The opening part of the second stanza is a good one to use as a mantra at night once in bed and before going to sleep. I say it with the Lord's Prayer. It can replace sleeping tablets. To surrender oneself to a loving God can lead to Peace of mind, comfort and it assists healing. The plea for help is granted.

Jesus repeated this psalm on the cross. It is also employed in some rites of anointing for those who are dying. In these rites the fragrance of the oils soothes and provides a reminder that paradise is near. It shows confidence in God as well as awareness of distress.

For those *'downcast in mind'* it is sad if punishment is expected from an angry God and even worse if undeserved through imagined or non-existent guilt. A church with too much emphasis on sin and not enough emphasis on the depth of His Love will not be the best comforter. The burden of depression can be very great for people with low self-esteem, with a high sense of guilt, or some other cause of black despair for which they may not be responsible. We can befriend them by listening with Love and encouraging self-worth as an urgent priority.

32 **Penance 2**
Forgiveness and Joy

Refrain ℟ *Souls pardoned by the LORD : sing*
out with JOY His LOVE and PEACE.

Blest is every soul,
forgiven by the LORD : when
sin is put away.
    When I did not admit my
    guilt : my health grew worse and worse. ℟

Troubled day and night,
I knew I must repent : the
LORD forgave my sin.
    All faithful hearts will pray to
    You : when they are in distress. ℟

'I shall be your guide
along the way : watch over
you and counsel you.'
    Sing out with JOY : since you are
    always cared for by His LOVE. ℟

At first it seems strange that Joy should feature in a penitential psalm. In fact sincere forgiveness and reconciliation is a source of deep pleasure. *'The practice of forgiveness is essential to our health and survival... It helps us to move on'.*[73]

To ask for forgiveness can be very costly and can cause deep pain.[74] A stubborn heart that will not forgive or admit to a fault causes trouble for all involved.

A dogmatic Church which lacks empathy does not allow comfortable growth. Rigid control of belief and searches for heresy make people feel anxious. Love, a key requirement for Christians and a middle way between dogma and freedom, is missing. A mature church, like a wise parent, will accept the need to explore without the need to condemn.

God knows this and understands our nature - He made us. He Loves us with unfailing Love and gives us self-esteem. Hearts who believe and trust Him find this in every-day experience. Those 'in tune' with Him, even if they come from a different faith, will feel His support.

I believe this is the sort of life we should aim to live every day; to allow Divine influence into our lives.

33   **The Believer's Ode to Joy**

Refrain ℜ   *Sing out your JOY hearts that LOVE*
           GOD : for all that He has done.

Sing with JOY to God
the LORD : all hearts that are in
tune with RIGHTEOUSNESS.
    With music praise the LORD : His
    WORD is truth, His works endure.   ℜ

GOODNESS fills the earth :
He made the Universe, His
breath became the stars.
    Let all on earth respect the
    LORD : He spoke and it was done.   ℜ

Bless-ed are the folk :
to whom He has revealed the
counsels of His Heart.
    He looks for those who trust His
    LOVE : He will save them from death.   ℜ

We have faith in God
the LORD : we serve Him for He
is our help and shield.
    With JOY we trust Your Name O
    LORD : it means that You LOVE us.   ℜ

The last psalm revealed the fruit of forgiveness is Joy. Here is the Davidic equivalent of Beethoven's Choral Symphony which puts Goethe's Ode to Joy to music. It is a secular poem, but it reflects the feelings of most human-beings.

It is more important to ponder on unity than divisions. We worship and pray to the Father in ways we can understand, not in ways we cannot. The same is true for people of other faiths.

Forms of worship vary greatly. All are accepted by Him. He knows whether our worship respects Him. He understands our divisions and receives everyone's prayers. Therefore I do not tell other people that their beliefs are wrong. If I am told mine are wrong I shall defend them. Dogma may threaten us as it threatened Jesus. We must respond as He did.

We say the General Thanksgiving *'for our creation, preservation, and all the blessings of this life ... for inestimable Love ... the means of grace and the hope of Glory'.* As we say or sing both this and the psalm, we can think of it as the Old Testament 'Te Deum'. We share it with all other members of the human race.

34   A Taste for God Brings Deliverance and Joy

Refrain ℜ   *Come taste and see GOD'S GOODNESS :*
if you wish a LIFE of JOY.

I will Bless the LORD
my God, my GLORY : meek souls
find He is their JOY.
    Come let us praise His Name : I
    prayed and He delivered me.   ℜ

JOY will radiate
from every face that looks to
Him : they are held high.
    His guardian angel watches
    them : and will deliver them.   ℜ

Taste and see the LORD
is Gracious : trust your LIFE to
Him, be filled with JOY.
    They speak the TRUTH, do GOOD, seek
    PEACE : and follow after it.   ℜ

RIGHTEOUSNESS will catch
God's eye : His ears hear prayer, He
will deliver help.
    All evil is destroyed : souls
    of all those who serve Him, saved.   ℜ

This is a special psalm. Each verse begins with a different letter of the Hebrew alphabet. As a group these psalms are about God's Goodness. Here the theme is deliverance and being saved. There are seven of these psalms and seven is a divine number.

The psalm is thought to relate to David's Life. He feigned madness to escape Abimelech. He was *'unsavoury'* in the Hebrew language. I do not believe that God will *'slay the ungodly'* but I do hope he will purge all their *'ungodliness'*. Then all that is good in them can enter heaven.

John Fisher is reputed to have repeated the second stanza while being led to the scaffold, behind which he saw the light of the sun.[75] He saw it as *'the true light, that lighteth every man that cometh into the world'* (John 1.9 KJV).

There is a second theme - taste. The words for taste and wisdom are related. *'Sapid'* means tasty, *'Sapience'* is Wisdom. We are asked to *'taste and see, how gracious the Lord is'*. Those who pray to fill their lives with God's Graces radiate his Goodness. To do so with humility gives encouragement.

35   An Appeal For Support

Refrain ℜ   *Blest Lord it gives You JOY : to*
                see Your servants live in PEACE.

Be my advocate O Lord :
say to my soul 'I will be
with you evermore'.
    May those who seek to kill my
    soul : be shown how to repent.   ℜ

Then Your angel will
show them the Way to walk : and
fill my soul with JOY.
    O LORD, who is like You : You
    save the poor from misery.   ℜ

Save my darling from
the lions : and my soul from
all calamities.
    In RIGHTEOUSNESS judge me O
    LORD : and vindicate my cause.   ℜ

My tongue will tell out
Your RIGHTEOUSNESS : and sing Your
praises all day long.
    Then all will know Your JOY : is
    when Your servants work in PEACE.   ℜ

The psalm refers to both human and Satanic enemies. Here Satan may be seen as the prosecutor and the Holy Spirit as our defence.[76] We have good reason to thank God for this Knowledge.

The angel mentioned could be winnowing the harvest. This process was done in a place where the wind could blow away the chaff and allow the grain to fall nearby. Separation of good seed from chaff is done gently. Here is another illustration of how the good parts of our nature could be separated from the useless ones. It is kinder than the silver seven times refined in Psalm 12 or Jesus' parable of the tares and wheat - Matthew 13.24-30. We hope He will be kind to us as well and save the good parts of our nature. We can act as guardian angels to other people and be kind to them as well.

'The voice of God is ... the lover who awakes in us what we cannot discover for ourselves.'[77] This is a feature of the best human relationships, including marriage. To observe God's Righteousness - consciously to do His Will with Love, for the benefit of human-kind, fills Him with Joy. The inevitable response is that He will give us a share in that Joy. Thomas Traherne referring to this psalm and the next puts it like this *'The judgements of God, His loving-kindness, mercy and faithfulness, are the fatness of his Love. His Righteousness being seen in the Light of Glory is the torrent of pleasure at His right-hand for evermore.'*

36   Human Failures, God's Virtues

Refrain ℜ   *Protect me by Your LOVE and*
TRUTH : lest pride takes hold of me.

Evil speaks to those
devoid of WISDOM : and with
no respect for God.
    They do not know Your LOVE and
    TRUTH : reach higher than the clouds.   ℜ

Like a mountain is
Your RIGHTEOUSNESS : Your GOODNESS
plumbs the deepest sea.
    You save both man and beast : we
    trust in Your abundant LOVE.   ℜ

We are satisfied
with generous feasts : we drink from
You the well of LIFE:
    And from that LIFE shines Light which
    bathes each human Soul in light.[78]   ℜ

LORD keep pouring down
Your LOVE on every soul whose
Heart's Desire is TRUTH.
    Protect me from all pride : and
    help those who feel cast aside.[79]   ℜ

This psalm was chosen by St. Benedict for Monday mornings at Lauds, the office said as dawn is breaking.

The psalm refers to *'the wicked'*, those who do not fear God, who flatter themselves and who believe their iniquity will not be found out. They plot mischief and deceit.

There is a plea to God to protect, guide and provide the strength necessary to resist these arrogant tempters. God's love is limitless, we can take refuge in it and we can feast on God's abundance.

There is a reference to the well of Life. It reminds me of Jesus at the well at Sychar. There He met a Samaritan woman to whom he offered water which would give Eternal life (John 4.14).

In our own lives we can make a positive resolution on Monday morning for the next six days of the week and ask for the *'true light'* of God's guidance in our week's activities. *'In your light we see light.'*

37   Deliver us from Evil

Refrain ℜ   *Fret not at rogues : trust GOD, seek*
GOODNESS, and you will find PEACE.

Do not fret about
those who do wrong : for they shall
wither like cut grass.
　　Trust GOD, act out His GOODNESS :
　　till the land and live in PEACE.　　　　　　ℜ

Find JOY in the LORD :
accept His Way and He will
give your Heart's Desire.
　　Trust Him : and He will make your
　　RIGHTEOUSNESS a guiding light.　　　　　ℜ

Hold still in the LORD :
anxiety brings sin but
humble souls find PEACE.
　　Through LOVE and charity, and
　　words of WISDOM : do His Will.　　　　　　ℜ

GOD LOVES RIGHTEOUSNESS :
when he directs your steps, He
lifts you when you fall.
　　He will deliver souls : whose
　　hearts pursue the Law of God.　　　　　　ℜ

The psalm takes the same view as that of Jesus when meeting social outcasts. Their way of life was an affront to the self-righteous but He accepted them.

An example is found in Luke 7.36-8.13. Jesus allowed a *'sinner'* woman to touch him in public and was pleased that she anointed Him. Even his very firm rebuke to Simon the Pharisee was gently delivered. Simon had put the Law of Moses above the loving Righteousness of God.

How should we react to wrong-doers? God is the one to take action, our job is to trust Him. We need to help those who are most affected by the wrongdoing - even if we are treated with derision.

Psalm 76.10 gives an important to clue how God will engage with the offenders. *'The fierceness of man shall turn to thy praise : and the fierceness of them shalt thou refrain.'* [80]

To have a mind that is at Peace with itself makes for 'wholeness', or Holiness, and is a healing process. It ensues from humility and 'doing what is right' to the best of our ability. This makes sound psychological and medical sense. It means there isn't any need to regret the past at a later date. Furthermore we are following Jesus' advice *'Take no thought for the morrow.'* We inherit the attribute of His Peace.

38   Penitential Psalm 3
Guilt 1
Jesus Prayer 4

Refrain ℜ   *LORD, chide me not : forsake me*
not : make haste to give me help.

LORD, rebuke me not :
my conscience pricks me, and
there is no health in me.
   My mind is overwhelmed by
   guilt : I cannot bear its weight.   ℜ

Heart's Desires have gone,
strength ebbs away : there is no
twinkle in my eyes.
   I am a leper : and there
   is no HOLINESS in me.   ℜ

Acting as if deaf
and dumb : words of reproach do
not escape my lips.
   In You O LORD I put my
   trust : You are my sure defence.   ℜ

I confess to my
misdeeds : and I have failed to
serve You well enough.
   O LORD forsake me not : for
   only You can make me whole.   ℜ

The psalm develops the theme of the last one, but here the ungodliness is that of the psalmist himself. The enemy is within, and it is accepted that sin is the cause.

An untreated facial cancer can be a shocking thing to look at. If this took place in Old Testament times it would have been regarded as leprosy; the sufferer would have been an outcast, with all the attendant physical and emotional misery aggravated by guilt. Recovery from any illness is hindered by all of those factors.

The psalm ends with an appeal for help and salvation. Again there are powerful reminders of the Jesus Prayer. God is not blamed but recognised as the one who will help him accept, or cure, the disability and make him whole.[81] We are God's servants here on earth. When we act to support people who are outcast by society we help to heal their bitter feelings as well as their 'disease'.[82]

39 Is There an After-Life? I Hope there is.

Refrain ℜ *Lord, save me from my sin : I*
hope that I may smile again.

I will watch my words,
while evil men are near : in
case I cause offence.
    I held my tongue although my
    heart was hot : at last I blazed.   ℜ

LORD tell me my end :
what is my LIFE about? Lord
am I right to Hope?
    In TRUTH my Hope is that : You
    will deliver me from sin.   ℜ

I do not complain
or grumble : GOODNESS will come
out of my distress.
    LORD hear my prayer : help me to
    hold my PEACE when under stress.   ℜ

Like my ancestors :
I am a passing guest of
Yours while here on earth.
    Give me some inspiration :
    so that I may smile again.   ℜ

There is no formal expectation of Eternal Life here and we find a heart that blazes with anger. In Psalm 51 there is a heart that blazes with a flame of sacred Love.

I have combined two verses in a way that does not appear in the original text. Hope, one of the things that will last forever, is mentioned twice. Liberties have been taken. They allow us to draw an analogy between *The Suffering Servant* described by the prophet Isaiah and Jesus before the High Priest and Pilate.

Christian behaviour should, of course, use Christ as the pattern to follow and we should also be mindful of Saint Benedict's prescription not to grumble.[83]

The Versicle *'Lord, in your mercy'* and the Response *'hear our prayer'* come from this psalm.

40   Prayer   Silence   Thanks
A Plea for the Future

Refrain ℜ   *I was serene while waiting*
            for the LORD : He heard my prayer.

I remained serene
while waiting for the LORD : He
heard my call for help.
   He drew me from a loathsome
   pit : and set me down on rock.   ℜ

He taught me to sing
'Give thanks to God' : that other
souls shall trust the LORD.
   Blest are all souls that trust Thee
   LORD : they see Your wondrous works.   ℜ

I exist to do
Your Will O LORD, my God : this
is my Heart's Desire.
   I have declared Your LOVE : Your
   TRUTH, Your RIGHTEOUSNESS and help. ℜ

Troubles hold me fast
I cannot see where I should
go : I need God's help.
   Deliver me, that I may
   Say with JOY : the LORD be praised.   ℜ

Above all in prayer one must remain serene. The difficulties and joys of prayer - particularly Contemplative Prayer are revealed in the psalm. The prayer of silence, listening to God, is never easy. Many voices, including our own, clamour for attention when our need is for stillness. Each of us must find our right way to respond to God at the present moment.

Candles, icons and/or crosses may help us to focus. With closed eyes, hold one of God's Graces in mind. If we become aware our mind has strayed, gently bring it back to that virtue while remaining calm and serene. It is important not to be angry with oneself. Christ has been a human being and knows all about the difficulties we experience.

There are times when the quietness and waiting seem to produce no reward. We can recognise our need of all that God has to offer but sometimes it is not clear what He wants of us. We feel there is something special He has in mind but waiting for it to become apparent may seem tedious. The immediate answer is self-surrender to whatever He ordains in the everyday events of our lives. Above all remember the words of Dag Hammarskjold, *'For all that has been, thanks; for all that will be, yes'.*

There are many times when we have reason to 'Give thanks to God'.[84] One way we can do this is by expressing thanks and Joy to those who help us. Saying 'That has made my day' will never go amiss. The direct thanks to God can be given at the same time or later during evening prayer.

41   The Beatitudes
Jesus Prayer 5
The Passion

Refrain ℜ   *O LORD show me Your Mercy :*
heal my soul for I have sinned.

Blessed is the soul
that cares for those in need : the
LORD will care for her.
    He will preserve her LIFE : and
    make her bed when she is ill.   ℜ

LORD be merciful
to me : heal me though I have
hurt You by my sin.
    My enemies detest me :
    my best friend has turned away.   ℜ

LORD be kind and raise
me up : spare me and I will
spare my enemies.
    In LOVE restore my health : I
    shall bless You for evermore.   ℜ

The opening verse reminds us of the Beatitudes, specially the first and fifth ones, *'How blest are those who know their need of God, the Kingdom of Heaven is theirs'* and *'How blest are those who show mercy, mercy will be shown to them.'* (Matthew 5).

The second stanza is a lovely precursor of the Jesus Prayer. The Greek word for mercy in the Jesus Prayer is also used in the parable of the Good Samaritan (Luke 10). We can see this practice of mercy in our own society. Those people who spend much time looking after the needs of others find that there are plenty of carers for themselves when afflicted.

Believers who are ill will see the Lord at work in everyone who cares for them. It is worth noting that a placid nature and a firm belief in recovery assist the human immune system.

In verse 10 of the Book of Common Prayer version of the psalm, the writer promises to *'reward'* his enemies. The Moffatt Translation uses to *'pay back'*. The psalm, as presented here, pledges that enemies will be spared. This is one of the cornerstones of Christianity – to love enemies. Dialogue, not war, is a keystone.

Refrain ℜ   *Have trust in God, gaze on His*
             Face : and you will smile again.[85]

As a thirsty deer
craves water : so my
soul needs You O God.
    I am athirst O God of
    LIFE : to gaze upon Your Face.   ℜ

I have had to drink
my tears when people say to
me : 'Where is your God?'
    I used to lead the people :
    to God's House with songs of JOY.   ℜ

Swamped in misery
and sunk by mighty breakers :
I am in distress.
    The LORD'S unfailing LOVE shines
    forth : each time I pray to Him.   ℜ

Enemies insult
me grievously : using
words that pierce my heart.
    The taunt they choose most often :
    'Has your God forsaken you?'   ℜ

This psalm and the next refer to exile in Babylon. They are relevant in times of distress. The enemies today might be disbelievers who challenge us or a personal lack of confidence.

Feelings of exile and misery are dominant. For us, the separation could have many causes; a new abode, old age or a severe illness. When we are ill many Christians feel removed from the Christian family meal, the Eucharist. The underlying message is to trust God, even when everything seems against us. Prayer should not be abandoned. If we look below the surface, there are many reasons to thank God and to smile.

Excerpts from this psalm appear in the liturgy for St. Mary Magdalene. The readings[86] all begin with a plea, with a sense of loss. Each time there is a positive outcome.

There are many references to water in this psalm. They emphasise that we die for lack of water but we can also can be drowned by an excess. Contaminated water spreads disease. Human beings are also both creative and destructive. We have a purpose in life to make the world a better place. Longing is not enough - we must act.

Jesus experienced thirst on the cross.[87] When we thirst for God we produce our best. He is close to us and He inspires us – we just have to ask.

Refrain ℜ   *O Lord send out Your Light and*
             TRUTH : to guide me to Your House.

Lord defend me from
ungodliness : deliver
me from wicked thoughts.
   Lord I am frantic : why not
   use Your POWER to give me help?   ℜ

Send out Light and TRUTH
to be the guides : that lead me
into HOLINESS.
   This is the House in which You
   dwell : and where Your altar stands.   ℜ

Thither I shall come
O God, my God : You are the
God of all my JOY.
   O my Redeemer : I shall
   praise and thank you on the harp.   ℜ

Why, my soul, do you
go heavily : and why are
you disquieted?
   Put trust in God, and gaze[88] on
   Him : then you will smile again.   ℜ

This psalm is very special. Saint Benedict used it during the Office of Lauds (praises) at dawn on Tuesdays. It refers to Joy and is still used by the Church on Sundays.

Priests say the psalm before celebrating the Eucharist and I use it in my own preparation for the service. 'Eucharist' means thanksgiving and its Holiness brings wholeness and healing to our minds and bodies.

- As I approach the altar I say Song of Songs 4.16 *'Come north wind blow, come south wind blow as well, that sweet perfume may fill the world.'*

- While at the altar I ask that all wickedness in me will be de-throned and that the Father will enthrone Himself.

- After leaving I repeat Isaiah 6.7-8 : *'This Holy food has touched your lips. It has removed your wickedness, and pardoned all your sin. The Lord then said 'Who shall I send?' and I replied 'Here am I, You may send me.'*

We ask to become the *'light set on a hill'*[89] a Light that will lead others to God. The *'holy hill'* and *'thy dwelling'* were the hill on which Jerusalem is set and the Temple. For us this could be our local church and the step to the sanctuary within.

The psalm reminds us of our own failings. All too often we don't do the good things we want to do and we end up going astray (Romans 7.19-20).

When ill and unable to attend church we can ask a priest to bring the elements to us wherever we are. This helps us to recover, to smile again, another way of saying *'the help of my countenance'*. To gaze upon God's face is Contemplation.[90] In Contemplation we see life's problems with God's perspectives.

Refrain ℜ   *O God You have confused us :*
yet You are our Heart's Desire.

We have heard O God
about our ancestors[91] : and
how You planted them.
    You helped them with the POWER
    of Your hand : You smiled on them.   ℜ

Lord, You are our King :
and in Your Name we
shall defeat our enemies.
    But now You are far off : You
    do not help, we are confused.   ℜ

We are eaten up
like sheep and scattered : laughed to
scorn and valueless.
    Our Heart's Desire is turned to
    You : and we still walk Your Way.   ℜ

Lord, for Your sake we
are being slaughtered : why is
Your smile hid from us?
    Arise and give us help : and
    in Your LOVE deliver us.   ℜ

At the start of the psalm we are reminded that God's people were 'planted' in Israel. Planting in itself does not ensure a good harvest - there has to be correct nurture. The keeper of the vineyard in Isaiah 5.2 thought he was looking after the vines properly but the end result showed he was not. The grafted part of the vines died, and only the root-stock yielding wild grapes survived.

The second stanza suggests a battle has been lost. The psalmist feels confused. Perhaps the confusion is part of God's plan. When it happens to us, are we being asked to question ourselves and our relationship with God? Thomas Traherne says *'The falling out of Lovers is the beginning of Love: the renewing, the repairing and the strengthening of it'.*[92] It is always good to have a discerning spiritual friend who knows our heart. It is as if we have been planted but we may need advice from the Head Gardener. We can also get help from looking at other psalms that deal with feeling separated from God - 10, 13, 22, 35, 88 and 109.

Pierre de Caussade reminds us that the present moment is always the ambassador of God. In it is everything that is necessary to achieve Holiness.[93]

The start of the last stanza is quoted in Paul's Letter to the Romans 8.36-39, which offers a positive response to persecution. Christians who escape this evil can help those afflicted, through prayer.

45   A Royal Wedding Song

Refrain ℜ   *I praise our King whose Word is*
GOODNESS, TRUTH and RIGHTEOUSNESS.

GOODNESS is the theme :
of all the poems that I
write about the King.
 Ride on in majesty and
 GLORY : girded with your Sword.[94] ℜ

Every word You speak
is Gracious : full of GOODNESS,
TRUTH and RIGHTEOUSNESS.
 Enthroned for evermore : You
 rule with LOVE and RIGHTEOUSNESS. ℜ

God anointed You
with JOY : Your bride is at Your
side, she worships You.
 I shall immortalise Your
 Name : the world will sing Your Praise. ℜ

Thomas Traherne, in his pursuit for Felicity, finds Joy in this and the next six psalms.

Psalm 45 is an Epithalamium, a poem to celebrate wedlock. For us it marks the marriage between Christ and His Church. The Bridegroom – Christ; the Bride – His Church, and the Palace – this World, are foreseen as David's Joy.

In God's eyes every male is a Prince over all the earth and every female is a Bride to the King of Heaven.[95] It behoves us to treat everyone we meet as a Prince or Princess. We should be courteous and respectful when talking about others, even in their absence.

The psalm can be seen as a model for married couples, and those intending marriage, as they work together with God to establish His Graces in the world. A home in which Love, Truth, Goodness, Righteousness and Joy are found is a source of well being. A happy marriage can have an infectious nature. Children born to such a union are likely to absorb the values of their home and to spread these in their own lives.

Refrain 𝕽   *'Be still and know that I AM*
GOD : I rule the universe.'

God gives us both POWER
and Hope : He is a proven[96]
help when in distress.
   We will not be afraid : though
   circled by catastrophe.   𝕽

Round His City flows
A river : it fills her with
HOLINESS and JOY.
   With God's support to give her
   early help : she will not fall.   𝕽

Men make war too much :
but when God's voice is raised their
Hearts of Stone will melt.
   The Lord of Hosts is with us :
   with His Heart of Perfect LOVE.   𝕽

You know LOVE makes wars
to cease : behold God's works bring
PEACE to all the world.
   'Be still and know that I AM
   GOD : I rule the universe.'   𝕽

If I remember only one verse from all the Psalms it will be 46.10, *'Be still and know that I AM GOD'*. It contains crucial links between both Testaments and our daily life.

Being still is the key to Contemplative Prayer. This calls for complete surrender of body, soul and spirit to God. The human body require twenty minutes rest before blood-pressure settles, and longer if we are anxious. Only God can take care of our spirit. When we surrender all to Him, He becomes our Home and the route to health and holiness.

In daily life, knowledge is key to trust. In religious life it is the Way to faith. We do the minimum and delegate the rest to God. Because He is within us He will come to our help *'and that right early'.* In our morning prayer each day we come face to face, making a fresh start, *'for every day may be the beginning of salvation for us, or through us for others'.*[97] We need to stop struggling and keep both mind and body as quiet as possible. Thereby we are re-created (Psalm 51).

'I AM' links the psalm to Jesus who used these words seven times in St. John's Gospel :

    6.35   I AM the Bread of LIFE
    8.12   I AM the Light of the World
    10.7   I AM the Door of the Sheepfold (NEB)
    10.11 I AM the Good Shepherd
    11.25 I AM the Resurrection and the Life
    14.6   I AM the Way the Truth, and the Life
    15.1   I AM the True Vine.

47   God's Kingdom Enthronement Psalm 1

Refrain ℜ   *Acclaim our God our King with*
JOY : and Praise His HOLINESS. [98]

Clap your hands : sing out
with JOY to God the LORD all
peoples of the world.
    The LORD Most High is awesome :
    greater than the kings on earth.   ℜ

He desires that all
the world should share His Glory :
as a heritage.
    He has gone up to Heaven : with
    music and with Songs of Praise.   ℜ

Praise Him, praise Him, He
 is King of all the earth : in
HOLINESS enthroned.
    His POWER is Supreme : He
    cares for everyone on earth.   ℜ

The theme of the last psalm is continued. God created every human being. We are all made by, and loved by, Him. All aggression must be put aside.

The psalm was used when Israel's kings were crowned, on their anniversaries and at the start of a new year.[99] Christians sing it on Ascension Day.

Compelling links are found between this psalm, the Lord's Prayer and the Hallelujah Chorus. In the Lord's Prayer we find *'Thy Kingdom Come'* and *'Thine is the Kingdom, the Power and the Glory'*. The Hallelujah Chorus has a memorable entry half way through *'The Kingdom of this world has become the kingdom of Our Lord, and of His Christ. And he shall reign for ever and ever. King of kings and Lord of lords.'* The first five words are sung quietly, the rest are very loud.

If you are like me, you may find that to say the Lord's Prayer can be automatic - you reach the end and wonder 'did I say the words and mean them?' A way round this is to say the whole prayer very slowly. One or more breaths are used for each phrase. They then become your Heart's Desire.

48   God's Invincible City.

Refrain ℜ   *O LORD, we re-enact Your*
LOVE for us : within Your house.

We show God respect :
His City, Sion, is a
JOY to all the earth.
   Most beautiful : and sited
   on the hill of HOLINESS.   ℜ

Kings who march toward
her are astonished : she will
never be destroyed.
   We know what we have seen : the
   LORD upholds her evermore.   ℜ

We shall re-enact
the story of Your Love for
us : within Your House.[100]
   Your Name is praised throughout the
   world : as is Your RIGHTEOUSNESS.   ℜ

Let the GOODNESS of
Your Word, and Your forgiving
LOVE : fill us with JOY.
      Tell children and grand-children :
      Let the LORD guide you through LIFE. ℜ

Psalm 48 reminds Donald Coggan of Jacob's ladder, a stairway from earth to Heaven; it came to him in a dream. He named the place 'Bethel, Gateway of God'. Spaces like those inside Cathedrals are, for him, 'thin' areas where one can sense the divine. People have hallowed them by prayer for centuries.

Sion of the Old Testament becomes Jerusalem in the New Testament. In Jesus' time politics and military power affected religion. They still do, but now three religions are involved. Judaism, Christianity and Islam all have Jerusalem as a focal point. Disagreement means there is a deep need for healing. We need to pray and work for the Peace of Jerusalem (Psalm 122).

Christians re-enact God's Love for us in the Eucharist. In some prayers we are asked to do so as *'our duty and our JOY'*. I see the Service as an invitation that I am delighted to accept.

Refrain ℜ　*Pay heed to words of WISDOM :*
RIGHTEOUSNESS will win the day.

Hear and ponder on
My words all souls on earth : whatever your estate.
　My mouth will sing with WISDOM :
　from the KNOWLEDGE in my heart.　　ℜ

Like a parable :
within the music is a
message you can hear.
　I shall not be afraid : when
　words of malice bite my heels.　　ℜ

Those who boast of wealth :
with their accomplices will
die like animals.
　You cannot buy Eternal
　LIFE from God : at any price.　　ℜ

RIGHTEOUSNESS will break
like dawn : a beneficial
presence in the world.
　God has redeemed my LIFE : He
　will receive me to Himself.　　ℜ

The enigma of life is considered by the psalmist. In spite of all the problems caused by those who are excessively rich, they will die, just like everyone else.

The psalmist knows in his wisdom that the wealthy cannot buy Eternal Life. God will deliver him from death. Righteousness here on earth is the key to the treasure of Truth, Peace and Joy. The Gelineau Version of the Psalms points out *'In his riches man lacks wisdom'*.

Knowledge of Good and Evil is basic to the human condition. Without it human beings behave like animals. The next psalm shows the action we must take – to honour God by giving Him thanks. As with the last psalm, we do this every time we remember Christ's death for us in the Eucharist.

Fundamentalist beliefs are narrow. They threaten souls who have a wider approach to Life. The Death Penalty is still used in some countries; it disguises fear.

Jesus takes away fear and transforms it into Love.[101]

50   **Our Chief Duty to God.**

Refrain ℜ   *Thank God and keep your word :*
            call Him when troubled, He will hear.

The All-POWERful GOD,
in Perfect Beauty : takes the
whole wide world to task.
   He calls the universe : to
   validate his RIGHTEOUSNESS.   ℜ

'O My people, hear
My words, I AM your GOD : all
is not well with you.
   Give thanks to God : respect the
   vows that you have made to Him.   ℜ

Call Me when you are
distressed : I shall save you and
you will honour me.
   If you disdain my Word : no
   other can deliver you.   ℜ

Practice honesty,
be pure : and speak the TRUTH while
using kindly words.
   Surrender to my LOVE : and
   walk with beauty and with Grace.'   ℜ

Beauty is a significant word early in the psalm and at its end. To *'order your conversation right'* (BCP) will mean that it is beautiful in the Sight of God. We are therefore filled with Joy and Love.

To find Joy in life inevitably leads to thanksgiving and praise. Thomas Traherne writes *'praises are the breathings of interior love, the marks and symptoms of a happy life'*. Part of my evening prayer every day is spent giving thanks to God for all the good things that have happened. Even on the worst possible day there is always something for which I have to thank God.

In the Eucharist we *'give thanks to God'* and receive spiritual food on earth - a foretaste of the heavenly food we shall be given hereafter. The mysterious word *'epousia'*, translated as 'daily' in the Lord's Prayer, can also mean celestial.

This psalm is important for Jews. It is the call to repentance on the Day of Atonement. For Christians in New Zealand this is an Advent psalm, calling for Justice (Righteousness) and Truth.

51   Penitence 4
A Prayer for Help
Jesus Prayer 5

Refrain ℜ   *Lord, in Your tender LOVE*
and GOODNESS : pardon my misdeeds.

In Your tender LOVE
and GOODNESS, Lord have mercy :
pardon my misdeeds.
    You placed TRUTH in my heart : teach
    me your secrets, make me wise.   ℜ

Wash me clean, as white
as snow and heal my bones : that
I may dance for JOY.
    Help me to teach Your Ways : to
    those who do not trust in You.   ℜ

Lord, deliver me
from evil thoughts : You are my
only source of health.
    Lord, open wide my mouth : that
    I may always sing Your praise.   ℜ

Recreate my heart :
to be Your Holy Spirit's
home for evermore.
    May sacred LOVE burn there : with
    inextinguishable blaze.   ℜ

This is a very, very powerful psalm. It is ascribed to David and the story is told in 2 Samuel 11.2-12.25. David arranged that Uriah should be killed in battle after he had made Uriah's wife, Bathsheba, pregnant. The death allowed David to marry Bathsheba which was wrong in the eyes of the Lord. Nathan the prophet made David condemn himself.

There is also a second very strong message – Divine Creation. There is a feminine side to God's nature. At the start we appeal to His tender Love. Later God is asked to *'re-create my heart'*. We pray for new life to be conceived in us.[102] The idea is explored further in Isaiah 66.7-12.

In different versions of this psalm 'Joy' appears in several places. Knowledge that you are forgiven lifts a great burden from one's heart. Thomas Traherne (Centuries 3.83) explains *'What more can melt and dissolve a lover than the tears of a returning friend?'* Allegri in his 'Miserere' sets this psalm to some of the most divine music ever written.

After I was given a new heart valve in 2005 I found my Heart's Desire was changed. I wanted my body, mind and spirit to conform to the Father's plan for me. Through the energy of the Holy Spirit I longed to become a Channel of Divine Power. I pray that, through Jesus Christ, I will be helped to work such miracles as He wishes while I am on earth.

Saint Benedict required that this psalm should be said every day, just before dawn.[103] Each day then begins with a blaze of Sacred Love in one's heart.

Appendix 1

RELAXATION EXERCISES

'Are you sitting comfortably? Then I'll begin.'
(Listen with Mother B.B.C. Home Service 1950-1960)

1 Entry into Prayer

Go to the place you have chosen.

Consciously spend time becoming aware that in this place God is present with you, waiting for you with Love.

Slowly, become still, comfortable, perhaps using awareness, or stillness exercises. Make a very slow sign of the Cross - either external or mental.

Spend time asking the Holy Spirit to help you to pray. Spend time speaking to God about your needs.

Gently turn your mind to the chosen focus of your Prayer time, and begin PRAYER.

2a A Stillness Exercise Having settled yourself comfortably and remaining perfectly still, start to use the following sequence, remaining silent when the stars (*) appear and being aware, increasingly, of your feelings. Breathe out and say:-

Be	still	and	know	that	I	Am God
Be	still	and	know	that	I	Am *
Be	still	and	know	that	I	* *
Be	still	and	know	that	*	* *
Be	still	and	know	*	*	* *
Be	still	and	*	*	*	* *
Be	still	*	*	*	*	* *
Be	*	*	*	*	*	* *
*	*	*	*	*	*	* *

2b My own version of this exercise includes saying one of God's Graces as I inhale. This is continued until there are no more words to use on breathing out. In this way Contemplative Prayer is achieved.

3 A Simpler Exercise

Keep very still and just say *'Be still'* or *'I am'*.

Breathe slowly, inhale with *'Be'* and out with *'Still'* and pause. This is the time your body will naturally stop for one or two seconds.

The following comment (source unknown) is helpful:
The Lord spoke to me and said
'My Name is not "I was"
Nor yet is that "I will be"
Instead it is "I AM".

BE STILL
AND KNOW THAT
I
AM
GOD
FATHER, SON, HOLY SPIRIT
OMNIPOTENT OMNISCIENT OMNIPRESENT
INFINITE ETERNAL
LIFE
LOVE
WISDOM
RIGHTEOUSNESS
KNOWLEDGE
GOODNESS
TRUTH
POWER
GLORY
HOLINESS
JOY
PEACE

The prayer is taken from *'Exercises in Contemplative Prayer'* by Hugh Bradford. Having used it since 1938, I personally recommend this form of prayer; its benefits are beyond all expectation. It is based on Psalm 46.10a. It forms a figure poem recalling Christ on the Cross.

The main feature is repetition of a single word - one of God's Graces – see *Cloud of Unknowing* and Rabbi Nachman of Breslov.

When the Prayer is used for intercession a special form may be employed. It is phrased so that the outcome is placed in God's hands and this guarantees success (see Psalm 25).

It is as follows :

[Name in Full]
IN THE NAME
OF
JESUS CHRIST OF NAZARETH
BE SET FREE FROM ALL
EVIL
AND BE FILLED WITH HIS ALMIGHTY
LIFE
LOVE
WISDOM
RIGHTEOUSNESS
KNOWLEDGE
GOODNESS
TRUTH
POWER
GLORY
HOLINESS
JOY
PEACE

This is based on Acts 3.6.

Appendix 2

FREQUENTLY ASKED QUESTIONS

1.   'Why does God Allow Innocent Suffering?'

Readers of Psalm 8 will have found an answer to two of the
questions that worry people most about Christian belief:
a. 'Why do we exist?'
b. 'Why does God allow evil?'
The question of suffering, and the next question: 'Why me?'
are much more difficult. The main reply each time has to be: 'I
don't know'. We can still have a guess. Here are some of my
thoughts.

We can follow three lines of reasoning relating to suffering.

1. We have been born into a world where animals eat other
animals. Fear and suffering are part of the natural world. As
humans we are born with bodies and minds that break down and
die. We are also born with free will and intelligence. Free will
means that we can use our intelligence to improve life for
mankind and the natural world, or we can choose violence and
destruction. If we are to have free will, God can only allow this
if we are free to oppose Him.

2. Genesis 1.31 tells us that that Creation was very good.
Jesus' life on earth ended in the one of the most painful, but
undeserved, deaths the Roman army could devise. It was very
evil. It was accepted of Jesus' own free will. Immense good for
the whole of humankind ensued. Through it, God the Father
showed us that His Power to change the impact of evil into
Goodness is Infinite. By surrendering to suffering and death we
become part of the Way that enables us to share Creation's

Goodness and Joy with our Creator. He retains ultimate control, hence His power to transform evil into Good, and to answer prayer. We know from atomic power the amount of physical energy in Creation is immense. Maybe that caused God Himself great suffering at the Big Bang.

3. The Quantum Theory seems inconsistent to ordinary minds. Things can be in more than one place at the same time. There are things we needed to discover but could not until recently, such as the Higgs Boson Particle. God, too, seems illogical. He is more than one Person. In the Trinity He is three, yet one. He also works miracles. If we are made in His image we too may be illogical and therefore have free will. The way our bodies work may offer a microcosm of the essential nature of God the Trinity. I believe we can work miracles too - when we cooperate with Him.

2.   <u>'Why me?' and the Eucharist</u>

When Jesus conducted the Last Supper He Took Bread, Blessed it, Broke it, and Gave it to the disciples. As he was going through the Passion He may have wondered 'Why Me?' Deep down he would have known the answer. Because He had been tempted Himself, He could help others when they were tempted. It is found in Hebrews 2.18. It was a time when He had been <u>taken</u> from everyday life as a carpenter, been <u>blessed</u> at His baptism and at the Transfiguration, His body was <u>broken</u> on the cross so that we might be <u>given</u> Eternal Life.

The parable about the Pearl of Great Price (Matthew 13.45-46) deserves consideration. Before a pearl can be worn as a beautiful ornament, an oyster has to experience irritation from a piece of grit, and then die. To give us the Pearl of Eternal Life, Christ had to suffer and die. If anything can help a Christian endure hardship, it is the Eucharist. Through receiving the Body and Blood of Christ we are given grace. This gives us the strength to embrace life joyfully and to endure challenges. It is the power of courage and love that may inspire others.

When a mother is in labour God has taken her body, in a manner that has been blessed by Him for procreation, her body is broken and her blood shed as the baby is born in order to give a new life to the world. Seldom does she ask 'Why me?' It is quite possible that the same sequence of events, taking, blessing, breaking, and giving, will happen to us too. At times of personal suffering we may ask 'Why me?' I try to offer it to God and ask that He will use it to help someone else's pain. This becomes easier if we make a habit of offering even minor mishaps to God asking Him to use then as well. For instance when we take a wrong turning when driving or someone else upsets us.

3.   How Does Intercession Work?

'Whenever we pray we must be prepared for an answer that places an obligation on us. A prayer is always a commitment.' (Quaker Yearbook 1995 2.29)

The Quaker quotation gives a partial answer to intercession, but for me there must be more than this. We may be called upon to help heal someone else, specially if we have prayed for him/her. One way that was suggested to me at a retreat is that God longs to heal the human race. We are on earth to do God's Will. The more we work in accordance with His plan for human-kind, the brighter the light we reflect from Him. Those

146

who resist His healing Power put a shield between God and themselves. When we pray for someone we are reflecting His healing energy onto that person. Any shield put between God and the unbeliever may be bypassed. It shines into hearts which deliberately shield themselves from God's direct influence, because it comes from an unexpected direction. The greater our own reflecting surface, the more energy reaches the sufferer. To be effective in intercession we have to burnish and polish this energy source through prayer.

Often we can become personally involved. Most people appreciate knowing that they are in our prayers. We are more likely to ask about their progress when we meet them in the street. As doctor I find it helps to be told where the problem is - cancer of the right breast or a broken left hip - then I can direct my intercession to the damaged area. I do not ask for a cure; I do ask that the person *'be set free from evil'*. Sometimes I command that this should take place *'In the Name of Jesus of Nazareth'*. Once I had an experience when I felt the need to pray vigorously for someone in the middle of the night, without understanding what was going on, and I responded. It turned out later that a crisis which was expected later, happened at the moment the urge to pray came. All ended with the best possible human result.

Sometimes we have to act correctly *' as if it were our nature'* not because we understand it.[104]

COPING WITH MODERN LIFE

1.   The Human Body and Stress

When we are subjected to severe anxiety we cannot cope. We behave as if we were a pint jug. All is well as long as no more than a pint is poured into it - we can manage a pint of anxiety. But if more than a pint is poured into it things overflow and there is a great mess - we cannot manage more than a pint of stress. Then strange events take over and the result is unpredictable. Normally well-mannered human beings behave in a way that is out of character. They may become unthinking, cruel, destructive, or depressed; some sort of disaster is likely to ensue. We can observe this in ourselves or other people.

There is a corollary to this. If we are so full of our own concerns, we have no room for God in our lives. He becomes superfluous to our needs – or at least the way we perceive them. We cannot turn to Him when in distress.   You cannot ask someone to help you if you do not believe in their existence.

2.   Breathing, Healing and Prayer

A report in the British Medical Journal in December 2001[105] studied a small number (23) of healthy people and assessed the effect of rosary prayer and yoga mantras. It looked at the results on heart rhythms and found them beneficial. Both reduced breath rates to about six times a minute.[106] This coincides with natural inherent rhythms and produces reduction in blood pressure. One conclusion of the article was that to use a rosary might be seen as a health practice as well as a religious one.[107]

To use the Jesus Prayer as advised is exactly the same and will therefore have the same effect. It is interesting to note that the Prayer Cord and hence the rosary, may have come from Tibetan monks – another east-west link.

When life is fast and confusing, meditation can be slow and healing.

AFTERWORD

Fourteen years ago I created a booklet with introduction, short extracts and comments on Psalms 1-20. There were about 16 pages in all. The booklet was designed for my grand-daughter, Emily, aged 13, to mark her Confirmation.

The work was finished the day before but was still in the memory of my new computer. I tried to print it. I failed. My logic was no match for computer logic.

In the end I had to say to the Good Lord, 'If you want Emily to receive this present tomorrow, help me today'. The conflict between the two types of logic was resolved and Emily received her gift.

Subsequent encouragement started me off on a major project. All the psalms will be covered. There have been many problems and setbacks but encouragement, both human and divine, boosted my morale. You now have Book 1 in your hands.

"I am so glad that you have shared your interpretation of the Psalms with us all and I hope I can use it to aid personal contemplation of the messages within each text. Thank you very much for taking the time to make this project come together. I'm sure this wasn't what you envisaged at the start but I think you can be proud of how far this book has come since its humble origins fourteen years ago. "

Emily Phillips, Grand-daughter

Acknowledgements

This book would not have been started without the help of three people - Eric Milner-White, Patrick Irwin and George Sidebotham.

Eric Milner-White, while he was Dean of Kings College in Cambridge, prepared me for Confirmation. He was also one of those who taught Divinity (Religious Education) at my school. During my last year there our homework each week was to read the Psalms and find the best reference to a given subject. He made a major impact on me, and on all who met him, and (through the Festival of Nine Lessons and Carols from Kings College) on the whole world. He saw the Church of England as a bridge between all Christian churches, East and West.

Patrick Irwin (PKI he liked to call himself) taught me Contemplative Prayer in 1938, using a privately published booklet by Hugh Bradford written in 1935. The first prayer in the booklet is based on Psalm 46.10a and provides the framework for all the others.

George Sidebotham of the Community of the Resurrection at Mirfield suggested I should write about my beliefs. I was a member of the Fraternity of the Resurrection and had to write an annual report of my progress.

Many other people have helped me including Emily for whom this book was begun in 1999. Sue Alwyn-Smith and my son, David York Moore, have both made valuable contributions.

Stella Maris, an artist with a background in education, has

been invaluable as an assistant – researching, typing, editing and illustrating the book.

A great source of encouragement has been Bishop Simon Barrington-Ward who has boosted my morale consistently from 1996 onwards. He has believed in the project ever since it started in 1999.

Most recently came the assistance of Professor Michelle Brown, Professor of Medieval Manuscript Studies at the University of London, a writer, broadcaster and international lecturer. We attend the same prayer group and her help in the final presentation of the book has been invaluable.

REFERENCE SOURCES

Book of Common Prayer   Collins Glasgow
Good News Bible   The Bible Societies Collins/Fontana.
                           London, 1976
Jerusalem Bible   Darton, Longman and Todd.
                           London, 1974
Jerusalem Bible, The Psalms for Reading and Recitation
                           Darton, Longman and Todd.
                           London, 1969
King James Bible
The New English Bible   Oxford University Press.
                           Oxford, 1970
Holy Bible New Revised Standard Version
                           Oxford University Press.
                           Oxford, 1995
Oxford Bible Commentary Oxford University Press.
                           Oxford, 2001
Psalms from Taizé   Mowbray. Oxford, 1983
The Psalms, Singing Version (Gelineau)
                           Collins Fontana Books.
                           London, 1973
The Quaker Yearbook, 1995

GENERAL BIBLIOGRAPHY

Mitch Albom *Have a Little Faith.* Sphere, London, 2010
Simon Barrington-Ward *The Jesus Prayer.* Bible Reading Fellowship,
        Oxford, 1996
Sister Wendy Beckett *Sister Wendy on Prayer.* Continuum, London, 2007
Hugh St. J. Bradford *Exercises in Contemplative Prayer.* Brighton, 1935.
        Privately published
British Medical Journal Volume 323, 22-29 December 2001, p.1446-8.
Charles Causley *Collected Poems for Children.* McMillan, London, 1996
Pierre de Caussade *Self-abandonment to Divine Providence.* Burns and
        Oates Ltd, London, 1959
Deepak Chopra *Reinventing the Body, Resurrecting the Soul.* Rider,
        London, 2009
Paulo Coelho *Life, Selected quotations.* HarperCollins, London, 2008
Paulo Coelho *Manual of the Warrior of Light.* HarperCollins, London,
        2003
Paulo Coelho *The Alchemist.* HarperCollins, London, 1995
Donald Coggan *Psalms 1-72 The People's Bible Commentary.* The Bible
        Reading Fellowship, Oxford, 1998
Roald Dahl *The Twits.* Puffin Books, London, 2007
R M French *The Way of a Pilgrim.* Triangle, London, 1986
T.N. Hanh *Living Buddha, Living Christ.* Rider, London, 1996
Abbot Christopher Jamison *Finding Sanctuary.* Weidenfeld &
        Nicolson, London, 2006
William Johnson *Silent Music.* Fontana, Glasgow, 1988
T Keating *Foundations of Centering Prayer and the Christian
Contemplation Life* or *New Seeds of Contemplation.* Continuum, London,
        New York, 2002
C S Lewis *The Lion, the Witch and the Wardrobe.* HarperCollins
        Children's Books, London
Nan C. Merrill *Psalms for Praying.* Continuum, London, 2007
Thomas Merton *The Inner Experience.* S.P.C.K., London, 2003
E. Alison Peers *The Complete Works of Saint Teresa of Jesus.*
        Sheed and Ward, London, 1946
Eugene H Peterson *Psalms.* Navipress, Colorado, 1994
Brian Pickett *Songs for the Journey, The Psalms in Life and Liturgy.*

Darton Longman and Todd, 2002

Phillip Pullman *Northern Lights (His Dark Materials).* Scholastic Children's Books, London, 2007

Brother Ramon *A Hidden Fire.* Marshall Pickering, Basingstoke, 1985

Brother Ramon & Simon Barrington-Ward *Praying the Jesus Prayer Together.* The Bible Reading Fellowship, Oxford, 2001

Richard Rhor *Falling Upward.* Jossey-Bass, San Francisco, 2011

J K Rowling *Harry Potter and the Philosopher's Stone.* Bloomsbury Publishing, London, 2011

St. Francis de Sales *Introduction to the Devout Life.* Burns & Oates, London, 1959

Cyprian Smith *The Way of Paradox.* Darton Longman and Todd, London, 1987

St. Teresa of Avila *The Complete Works of Saint Teresa of Jesus.* Sheed & Ward, London, 1946

Thomas Traherne *Centuries.* The Faith Press, London, 1963

Unknown *The Cloud of Unknowing.* Edited by Justin McCann Burns and Oates, London, 1952

Norvene Vest *Preferring Christ.* Anthony Clarke Books, 16 Garden Court, Wheathampsted, Herts. AL4 8RF, 1991

C Wesley *Hymns Ancient and Modern Standard.* Hymns Ancient and Modern Ltd, 13a Hellesdon Park Road, Norwich NR6 5DR

Charles Williams *All Hallows' Eve.* Faber, London, 1945, 1st Edition

H.A Williams *True Resurrection.* Mitchell Beazley Ltd, London, 1972

Tom Wright *The New Testament for Everyone.* S.P.C.K. Publishing, 2011

William P Young *The Shack.* Hodder & Stoughton, London, 2008

William P Young *Cross Roads.* Hodder & Stoughton, London, 2012

END-NOTES

1   The Tablet, 24 October 1998.
2   T.N. Hanh, a Buddhist monk, *'Living Buddha, Living Christ'*.
3   Colossians 3:12-17 lists many of these Graces.
4   See Ezekiel 37.9.
5   Luke 2.35a '... *a sword will pierce your own soul too* ... '.
6   C S Lewis *The Lion, the Witch and the Wardrobe*; J K Rowling *Harry Potter and the Philosopher's Stone*.
7   Thomas Traherne *Centuries* 1.31 ... *'You never enjoy the world aright, till you so love the beauty of enjoying it, that you are covetous and earnest to persuade others to enjoy it'*.
8   In Paulo Coelho's *Manual of the Warrior of Light* bad things are used to bring good ones into the foreground.
9   Excerpted from *The Cloud of Unknowing* Chapter 7.
10   The Spirit is female in Hebrew, Greek *(psyche)*, and Latin *(anima)*. William Young's novel *Crossroads* calls Spirit *Grandmother*, but in *The Shack* her name is *Sarayu* - the Sanskrit word for 'wind'. In Hebrew, 'spirit', 'wind' and 'breath' are the same word.
11   A problem can arise. What do you do if the 'phone rings? I like to think that it might be Jesus at the other end - so I answer. This also makes me more courteous when answering at other times.
12   The first instruction T.N. Hanh (a Buddhist monk) received was to breathe in and feel calm; to breathe out and smile. It is difficult to think about smiling without doing it.
13   He compiled the Carthusian rules in 1127.
14   The 'Way of Understanding and Love' is the Buddhist 'Law' - Dharma.
15   *The Way of a Pilgrim* gives instruction on breathing. These are printed in Appendix 2.
16   The Greek word used here is one that means *to miss the target* or *not to hit the bulls eye.*
17   Simon Barrington-Ward, *The Jesus Prayer.*
18   BBC World Service 4 February 2012 at 13.30 pm.
19   The first Principle of Tertiary Franciscans is to make the Name of Jesus known and loved everywhere. The Second is to encourage a spirit of Love and harmony between all members of the human race.
20   *The Inner Experience.*
21   Cyprian Smith *The Way of Paradox.*

22   Matthew 5:3-12.

23   John 18.15-27.

24   John 21.15-17.

25   This interpretation gives a profound Passion-tide and Easter meaning to Psalms 22.22 and 85.10, as foreshadowed by Jesus' words at His Baptism (John 3.15).

26   The Roman scourge was designed to cause severe lacerations.

27   *'furiously'* gave voice to his anger, would be in keeping with verse 1. (BCP)

28   Paulo Coelho bases the story on this theme in *'The Alchemist'*.

29   Book of Common Prayer - the Prayer of Humble Access.

30   It can remind us of the final Resurrection, especially if our last thoughts each night are based on God c.f. Psalm 4.

31   Saint John of the Cross; *Silent Music* by William Johnson; the Introduction. See also Ephesians 5.19b '*...sing and make music in your hearts ... '* (NEB)

32   v.8 'Today if you will hear His Voice, harden not your hearts.'(BCP)

33   Other Psalms to be said at this time are 31, 91 and 134, with a versicle and response from Psalm 17.

34   Paulo Coehlo *Manual for a Warrior of Light.*

35   Precursors of the Jesus Prayer will be found e.g. Psalms 6.2, 25.10, 31.1, 41.4, 51.1. See Introduction.

36   The phrase is used by bell ringers at the start of each peal. c.f. Ps. 123.2 and comments on Ps. 27.

37   The questions 'Why do we suffer?' and 'What happens after death?' are ones that torment many people. Those whose suffering is great, and those who care for them, have the most distress. Psalms 8 onwards and 22 deal with this at greater length. See also Appendix 1.2.

38   H.A. Williams *True Resurrection* 1.6. See also Psalm 8 onwards.

39   The Greek word *metanoia* - 'a change of mind' applies.

40   I used to be a student silver-smith. In one piece I made an obvious mistake. My teacher showed me how to change it so that it became a handsome decoration.

41   Genesis 1.31 AV & Psalm 118. 24

42   Care for the environment will become a recognised Christian duty during the 21st century.

43   *Have a Little Faith* by Mitch Albom.

44   *Living Buddha, Living Christ.*

45   Brian Pickett *Songs for the Journey.*
Ernesto Cardenal transcribes vv 15-18:
'*Smash their secret police, O Lord ...*
That their military might may vanish without trace.
You are the one who reigns for centuries.
You hear the prayer of the humble and the weeping of the orphans. '

46   Reith Lecture No. 1, 2011. In this lecture, and on this point, she was talking about her detention under house arrest by Burmese generals over a period of 15 years and being unable to visit her dying husband.

47   C Wesley: '*O Thou who camest from above.* ' Hymns Ancient and Modern Standard 698. '*Upon the ungodly he shall rain snares, fire and brimstone, storm and tempest : this shall be their portion to drink'* (BCP). See also Psalm 83.13-17.

48   Paulo Coelho, '*Ever since time began, people have recognised their true Love by the light in their eyes.* ' *Brida.* Quoted from '*Life*'. See 34.35, when the face of Moses glowed so brightly after he and the LORD had gazed upon each other's face. Moses used a veil over his face.

49   T.N. Hanh.

50   T.N. Hanh.

51   Isaiah 6. 6-8 - this is part of my own meditation after receiving the bread and wine at the Eucharist.

52   Bettany Hughes. Huw Weldon Memorial lecture 18 October 2011 '*The practice of forgiveness is essential to our health and survival. ... It helps us to move on.* '

53   The Times, 2 July 2011.

54   William P. Young *Cross Roads.*

55   Usury means excessive interest. I am suggesting that it is lent interest free.

56   Philippians 1.9 & 4.8-9.

57   *True Resurrection* Mitchell Beazley Ltd. London, 1972.

58   c.f. Luke 11.4.

59   This phrase comes from a letter received after my wife, Helen, had died.

60   *Songs for the Journey.* See Psalm 95.8, where I have changed the words in a positive way. '*Today, should you hear His voice* ' becomes '*Be sure to hear : the 'Silent Music' of His voice today* ' as part of Daily Prayer.

The phrase comes from St. John of the Cross.

61   One possible meaning of *Aletheia* - the Greek for Truth - is *'with the right motives'*.   Sister Wendy is succinct on this point *'... Each of us is here to worship God for what He is, not what we can get out of our worship'* (*Sister Wendy on Prayer*).

62   Richard Rhor *Falling Upward, 'Humans are creatures of meaning, and finding deep meaning in our experiences is not just another name for spirituality but it is also the very shape of human happiness.'*

63   *Songs for the Journey.*

64   He finds great Joy in v. 22 - end: *'Ye that fear the Lord, praise Him ... A seed shall serve Him. It shall be counted to the Lord far a generation. They shall come and declare His righteousness to a people that shall be born, that He has done this.'*

65   *The Little Flower of Saint Francis* Chapter 7 *'Saint Francis writes that patience is the source of perfect joy'*.

66   BCP *'He shall convert my soul'*.

67   'Comfort' originally meant *'to supply with strength'*.   To em-POWER is a good alternative idea.

68   This oil is available at times of illness, not just for terminal disease. Early Christians used it freely.

69   SJ.

70   BCP.

71   Psalm 46.10.

72   JBR.

73   Bettany Hughes. Huw Weldon Memorial lecture 18 October 2011.

74   William Young *Crossroads*.

75   TP.

76   Romans 8.26-27.

77   S. J. p. 37 on verse 28.

78   c.f. John 1.9.

79   see Psalm 43.

80   BCP.

81   See comments on Psalm 39 vv. 10-13.

82   In the writer's case it is to correspond with a prisoner on Death Row in Florida.

83   Rule of St. Benedict 4.39, 5.19, 6.1 and 40.9.

84   The motto of the Girdlers' Company, one of the Livery Companies of

the City of London.

85   Transcription based on *Psalms* Eugene H Peterson (*THE MESSAGE* Navpress, Colorado Springs 1994).

86   The others are Song of Songs 3:1-4 and John 20.1-2,11-18. The St. Mary Magdalene liturgy is on 22 July.

87   John 19.28.

88   See Exodus 24.11 (JB).

89   Matthew 5.14-16.

90   SJ.

91   The Seder (Passover)Feast is still observed in Jewish households. Children ask special questions and the story of the flight from Egypt by the Israelites is told.

92   Centuries 3.83.

93   Excerpted from Chapter 10 *Self Abandonment to Divine Providence.*

94   *The Sword of the Spirit;* Ephesians 6.17.

95   Thomas Traherne, excerpted from Century 3.77.

96   NRSV footnote: '*well proved*'.

97   SJ.

98   Power to Heal.

99   2 Samuel 6.14-15.

100   '*within the womb of Your temple*' *Songs for the Journey.*

101   Psalm 76.10 BCP.

102   SJP.

103   See Chapters 13 and 14 of the Rule of Saint Benedict. It is also used by Jews to usher in the Day of Atonement - Yom Kippur.

104   c.f. Lyra in Phillip Pullman's *Northern Lights*, the first book of the trilogy *His Dark Materials.*

105   British Medical Journal Volume 323, 22-29 December 2001.

106   Ideally one should breathe in for a count of five (seconds), out for four (seconds) and rest, without movement for a further second.

107   The B.B.C. programme, '*The Truth about Personality*', confirmed this observation, (BBC4, 10 July 2013, 9 p.m.).